San Francisco's Mosaic Walls

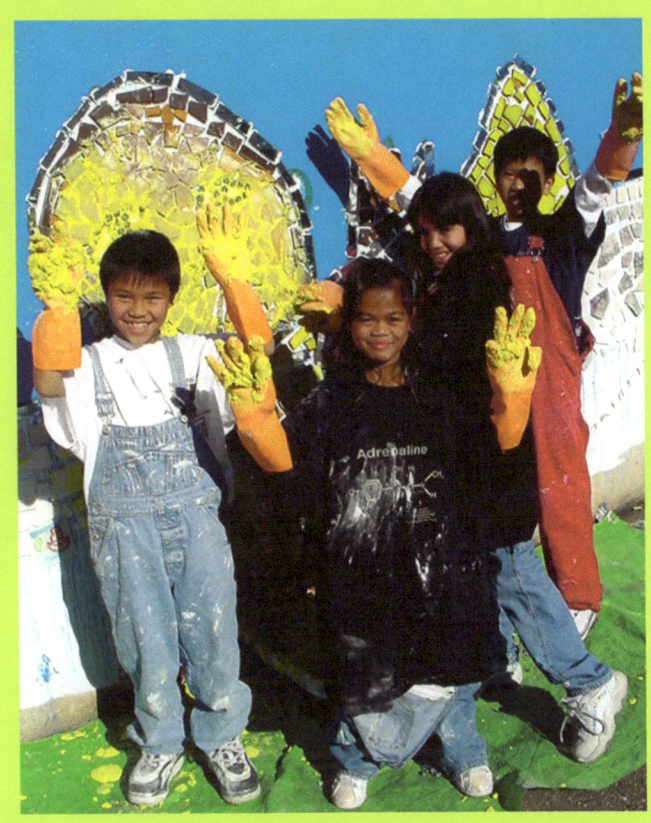

The Public Art of Josef Norris and Kid Serve

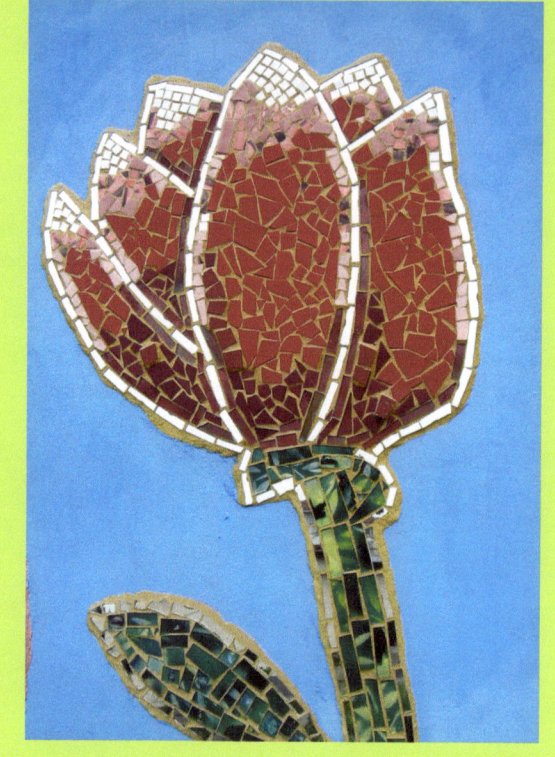

Cover: "Children's Botanical Garden" 2007
at 651 6th Avenue in San Francisco

Back: Detail from "Suncatchers" 2002
At 299 Oneida Street in San Francisco

First edition, 2007

Text and Photographs © 2007 by
Josef Norris
www.josefnorris.com

ISBN 978-0-6151-6128-0

Any findings contained herein are not necessarily those of the California Arts Council or the National Endowment for the Arts

Published by Josef Norris / Kid Serve
1068 Bowdoin Street
San Francisco, CA 94134

www.kidserve.com

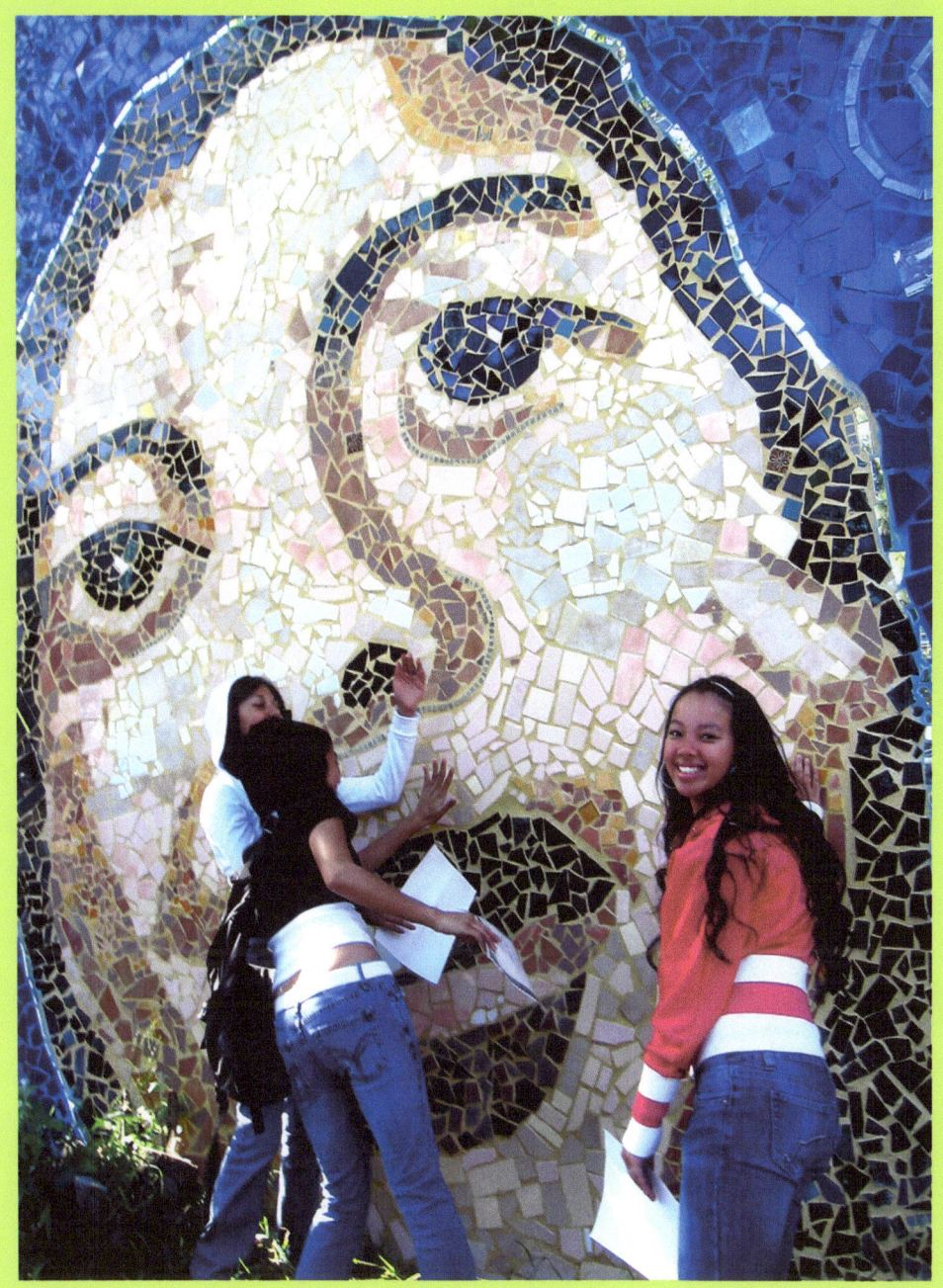

Introduction

I began doing murals as a way to get my art seen by a larger audience. Something happened along the way. While working on a mural, people from the community came up and started talking to me. They would talk about the mural, and what it meant to them, but also about the neighborhood, its history and ultimately about themselves. By the time I had completed the job, the mural no longer belonged to me- it belonged to the neighborhood, and I had made many new friends.

I began doing murals with children as a way to make extra cash to support my own art. Something happened along the way. Over the course of the semester, I got to know the kids. I became friends with the teachers and principals and saw the heroic work they were doing in inner city schools. Many of the teachers I know work under the most difficult of circumstances and are deeply committed to trying to reach their students and make a difference in their lives.

I run an arts education program in desperately poor schools in one of the richest cities in the country. I have personally seen schools shut down due to rat problems, and schools with no heat during the winter. I have worked in schools lacking books, paper, librarians, a school nurse, and balls for the playground. Many schools in San Francisco are segregated along racial and economic lines.

In 1999, while working on a large painted mural for the City of San Francisco, I answered an ad to lead a group of high school students through a one-week mural workshop. At first there was resistance toward a mural by young people - because the neighborhood had so many problems with graffiti. But when the kids were out on the mural site, removing the graffiti and painting their mural, several neighbors came out with water and snacks, congratulating the young artists on their work.

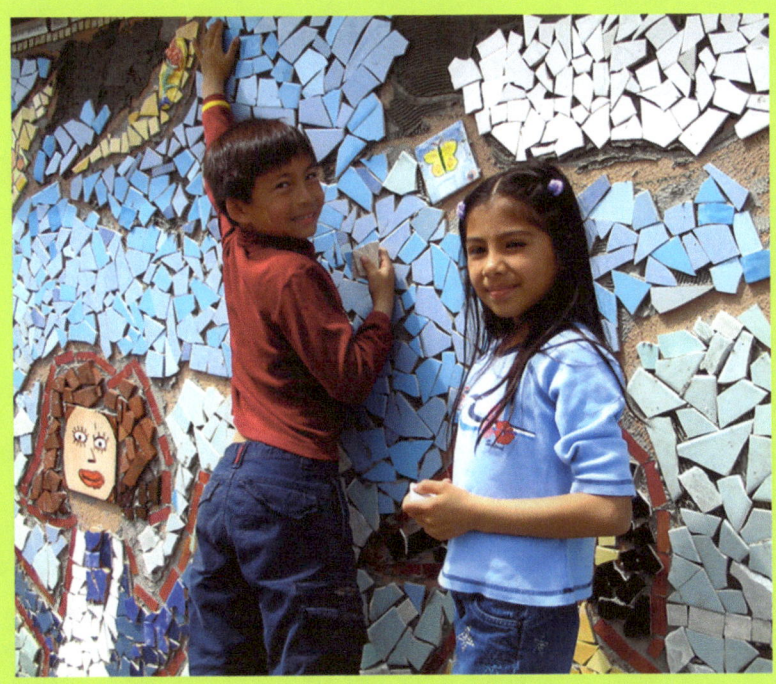

This success led to more partnerships and longer projects. We quickly developed 14-week residencies that were set up to be comprehensive partnerships with one teacher and his/her class. As an arts educator I was pushed to use creative muscles I didn't know I had. In an effort to reach more students I learned to work with mosaics.

Since 1999, we have supervised over 60 murals created by young people. Since 2002, we have done many of these murals in mosaics. Remarkably, only three of the murals have been vandalized. In those three cases, we removed the tags quickly and the graffiti did not come back.

All of Kid Serve's murals are outside and visible to the public. In the last 8 years I have seen many of the young Kid Serve artists grow up. Their murals remain.

Josef Norris
Director and Founder of Kid Serve

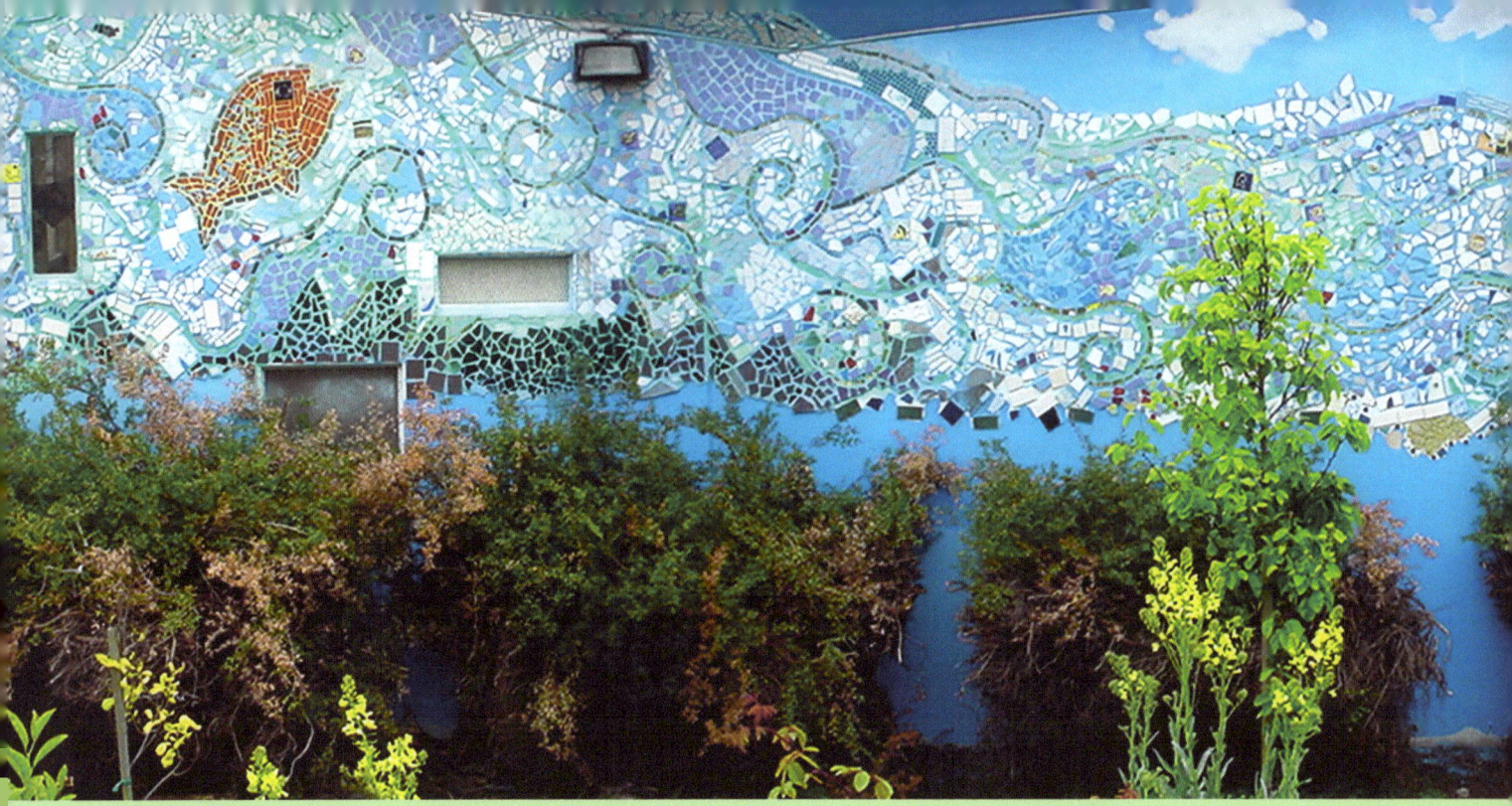

Suncatchers - **The First Mosaic Mural**

By 2002 I had been doing painted mural workshops in the schools for 3 years. I was eager to explore new ways of making art. I had heard about an artist who had done mosaic murals all over Philadelphia. While on a trip to Philadelphia a few months later I had a chance to finally meet Isaiah Zagar and got the courage up to ask him to teach me how to do mosaics - the Isaiah way. "Give me two days," he said, "I'll teach you enough to get started!"

In two days of non-stop work, I got an intensive course in his way of doing public art, which breaks a lot of rules, and is a wonderful way to learn mosaics. At one point I was meticulously figuring out which tile to put in its particular place and he stopped me. "Don't think about it too much," he said, handing me a random bucket of tile. "Just lay the tile and don't let your brain get in the way." Over the years, Isaiah has worked with hundreds of young artists who go on to create their own mosaic murals all over the world.

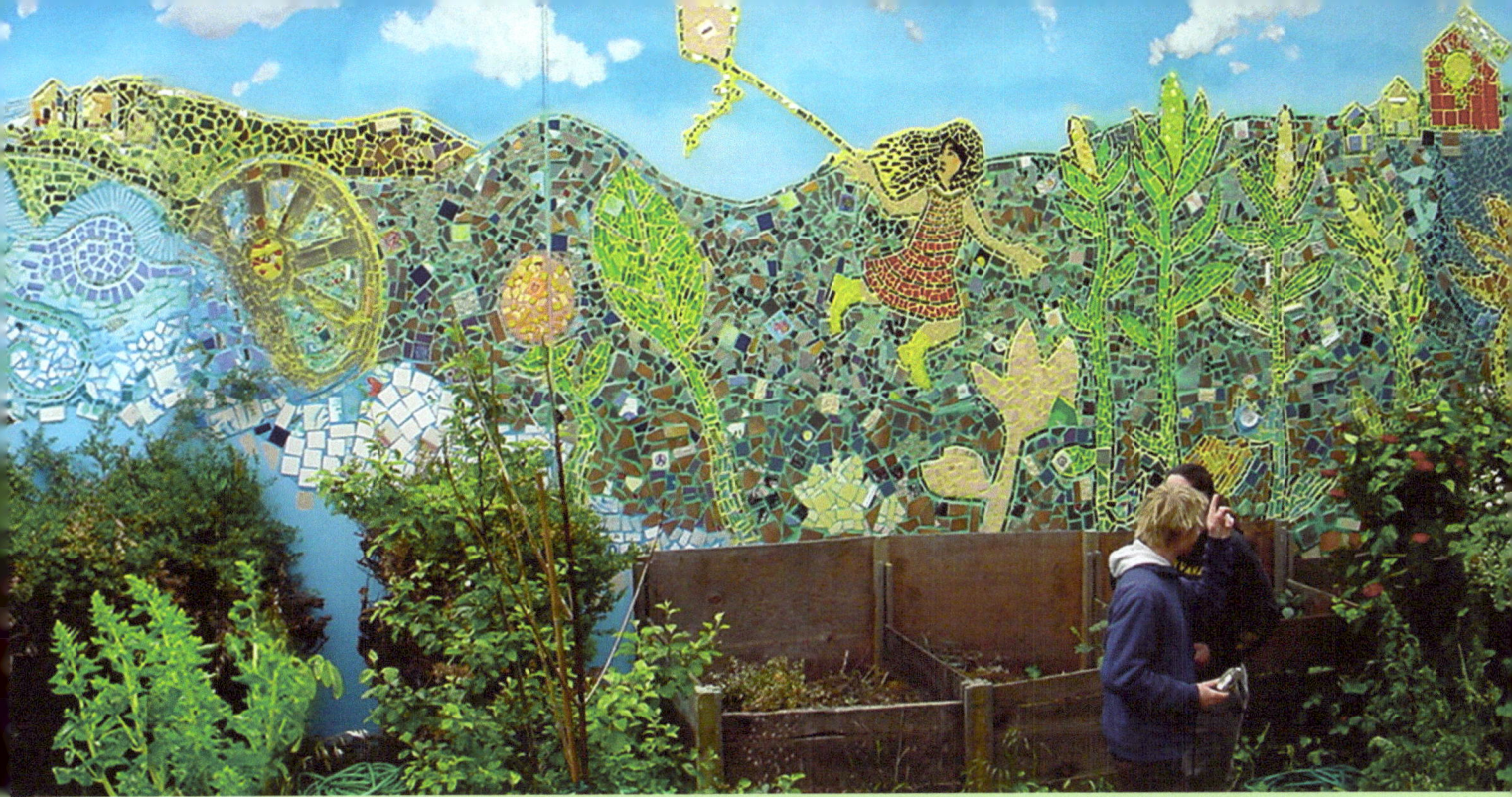

Inspired by my two days with Isaiah, I came back to San Francisco and created "Suncatchers" with a 7th grade class at James Denman Middle School in San Francisco's Southeastern Excelsior district. The outdoor space was a fenced in area next to the middle school that for decades had been used as a dumping ground for old desks and rusted file cabinets. Ten years before, a community gardening organization called "A Living Library" changed the junk yard into a garden.

Students grew, and harvested plants, and learned botany and science while being stewards of the land. This struck me as a perfect community partnership, because in essence we were working towards the same goal of bringing together young people to transform urban space.

Working with the gardening group, several volunteers, and an environmental youth group, we created this enormous mosaic garden over the course of six weeks in April and May of 2002. I found that working with mosaics, I reached an entirely new population of kids. Kids who swore they didn't know how to draw thrived on this project.

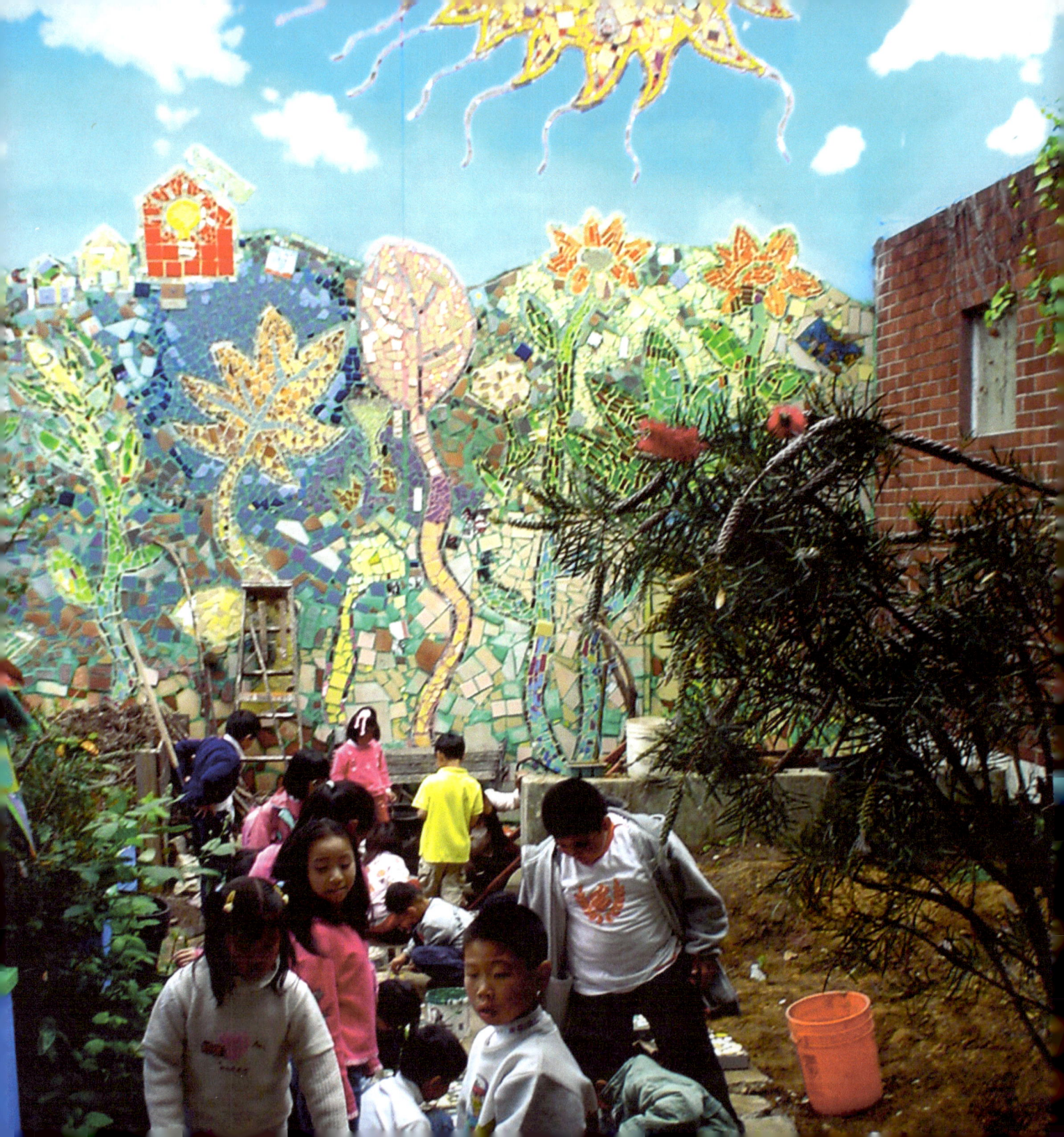

We used many of the techniques that I learned from Isaiah. The figures were outlined with cut mirror. We colored the grout different colors to help separate the figures in the foreground from the background.

When the sun shined on the mural, light would bounce off the mirrored outlines and project glistening patterns over the garden. These patterns of refracted light would change, depending on the time of day. The effect was magical.

When we took the scaffolding down, I was awe struck. I knew we had created something extraordinary and that I would never look at public art the same way again.

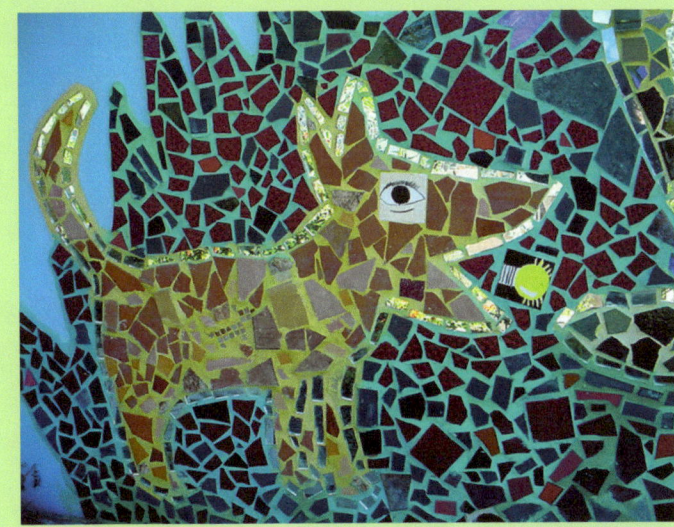

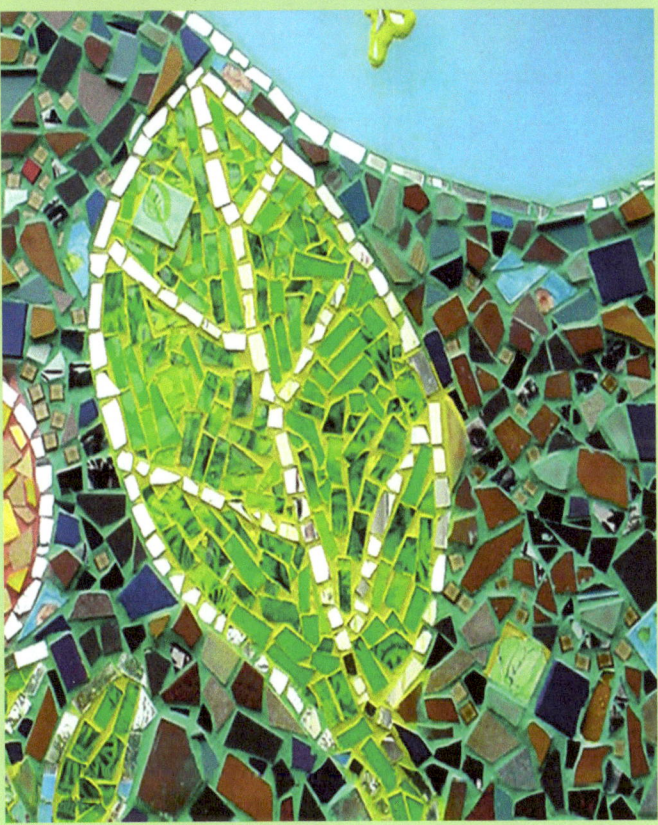

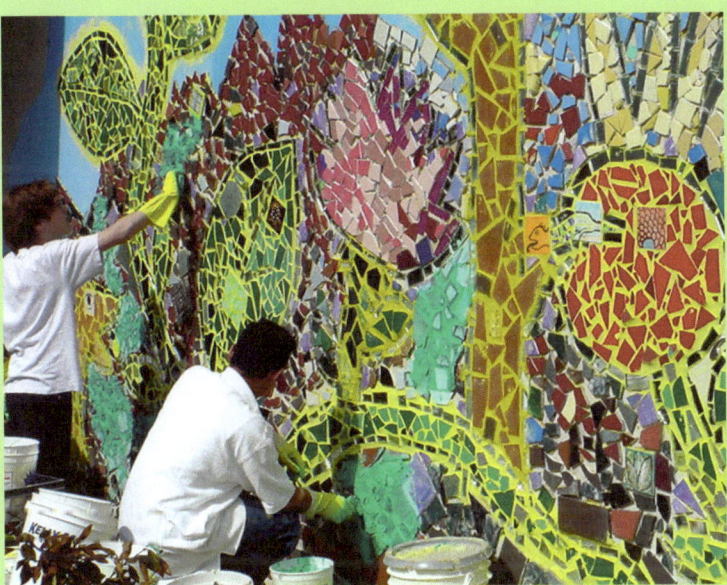

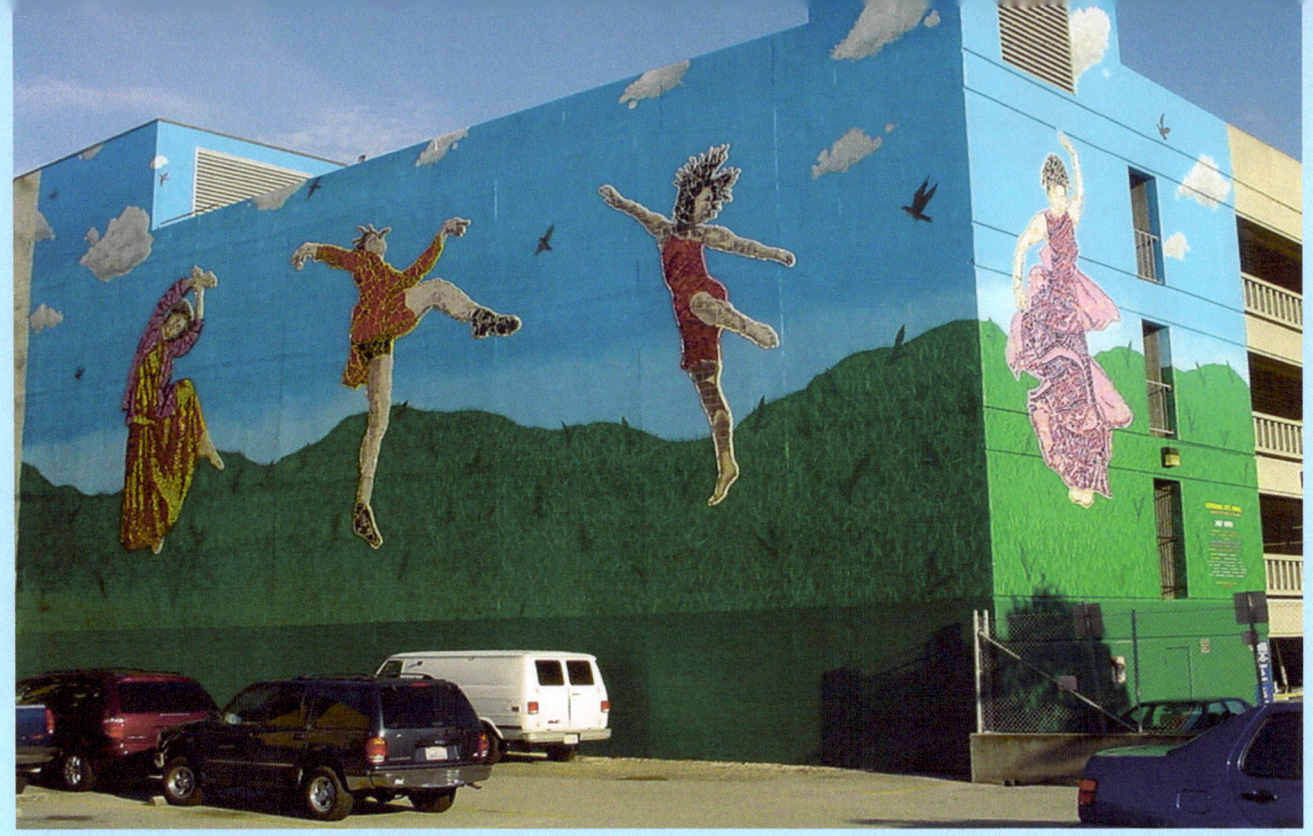

Mosaic Murals and Space

Mosaic murals challenge us to think about how we perceive our surroundings. With paintings or photographs we have to get closer to get a better look. With mosaic murals, we have to get farther away to see them more clearly. From a distance a mosaic mural can look painterly; up close the same mural can look like a work of abstract expressionism, filled with hundreds of personal details. Murals are different from paintings in a gallery, in that they are placed in urban environments where people are always moving - walking, cycling or driving from one place to another. Because light interacts with each piece of tile differently - when you're walking around a mosaic wall the mural actually glistens.

The "Performing Arts Mural" faces oncoming traffic driving down a one-way street. Because most people see this mural from a moving car, I chose to outline the figures in mirror, giving the impression that the dancers are in a state of constant motion.

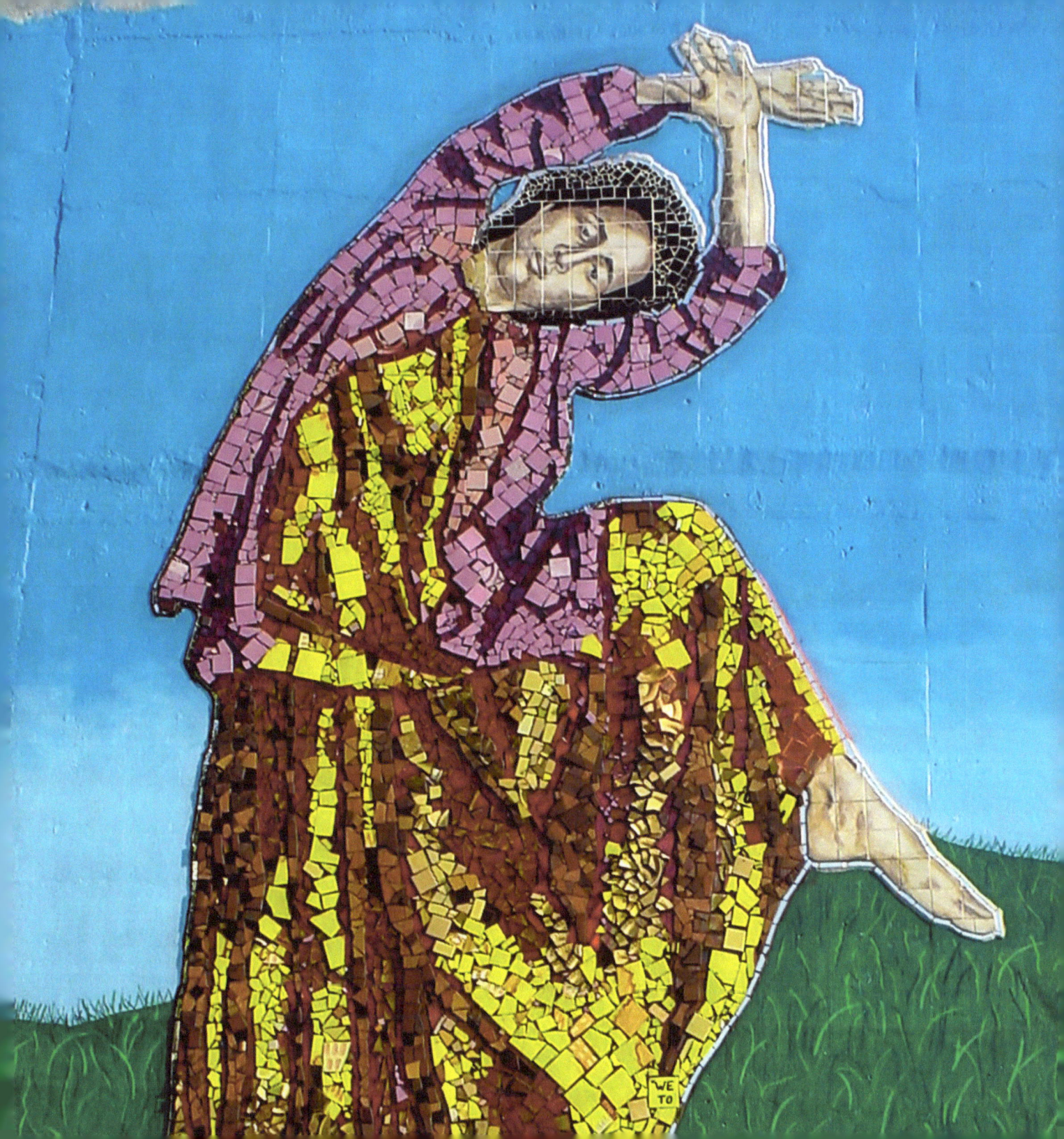

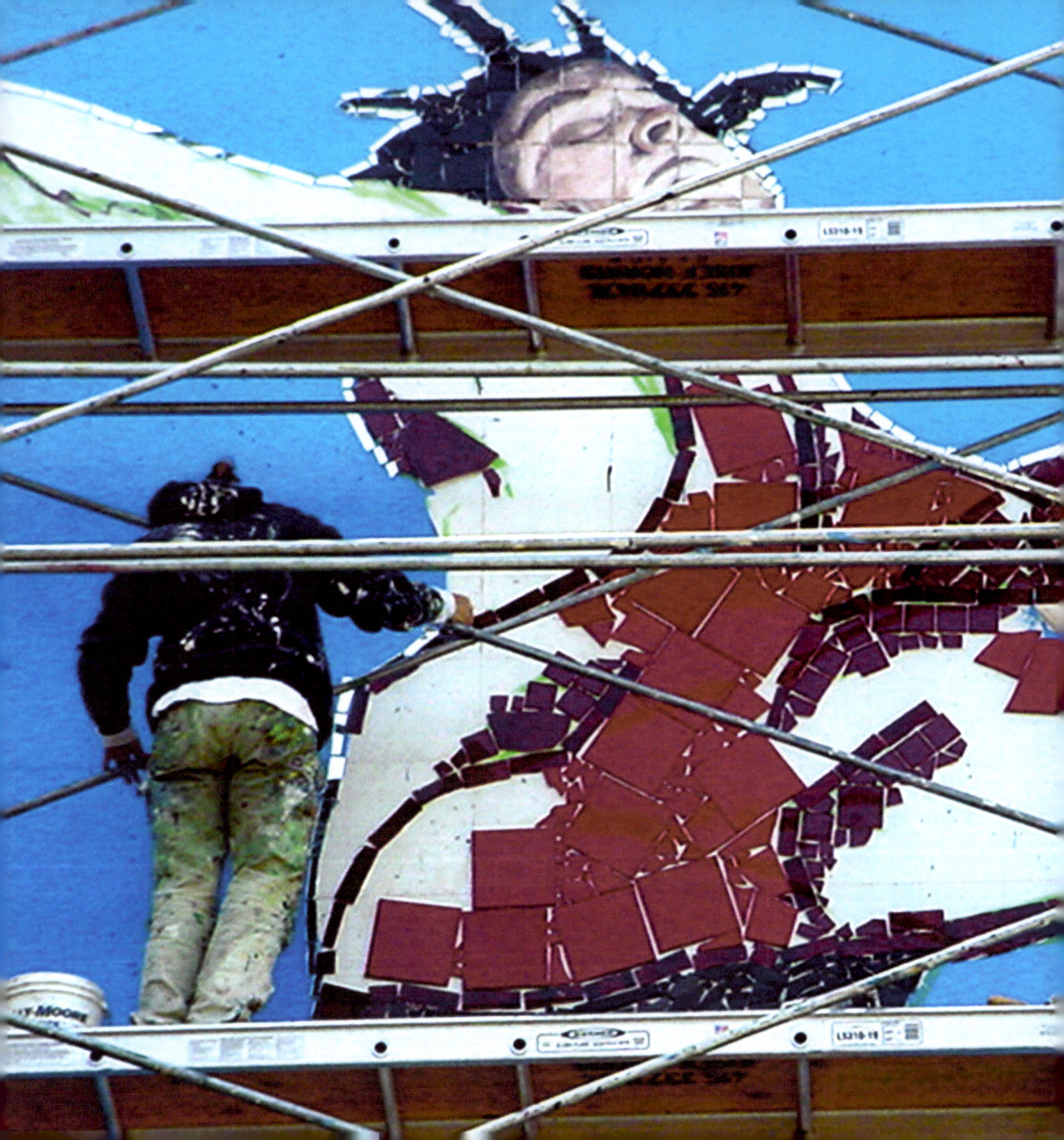

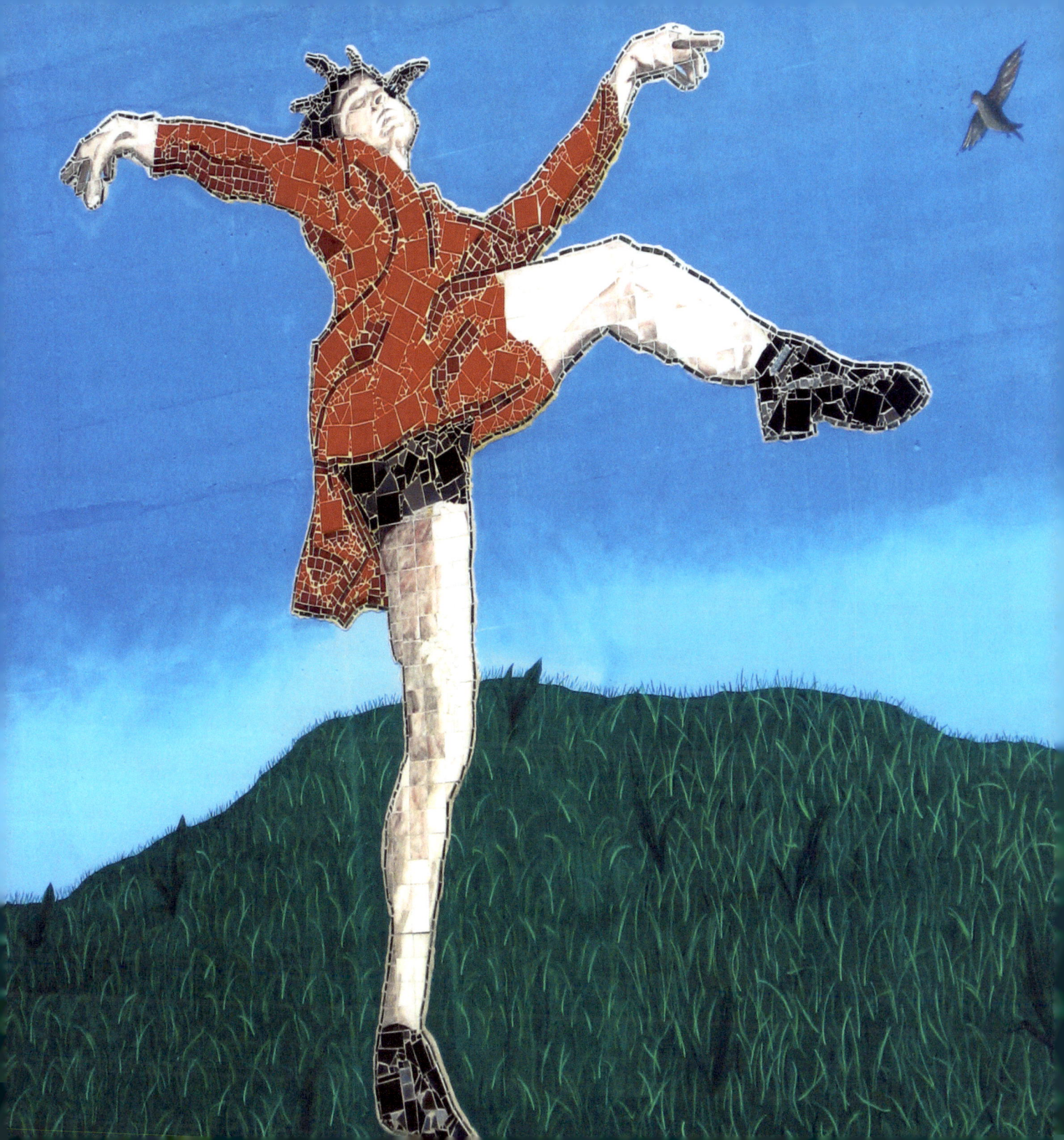

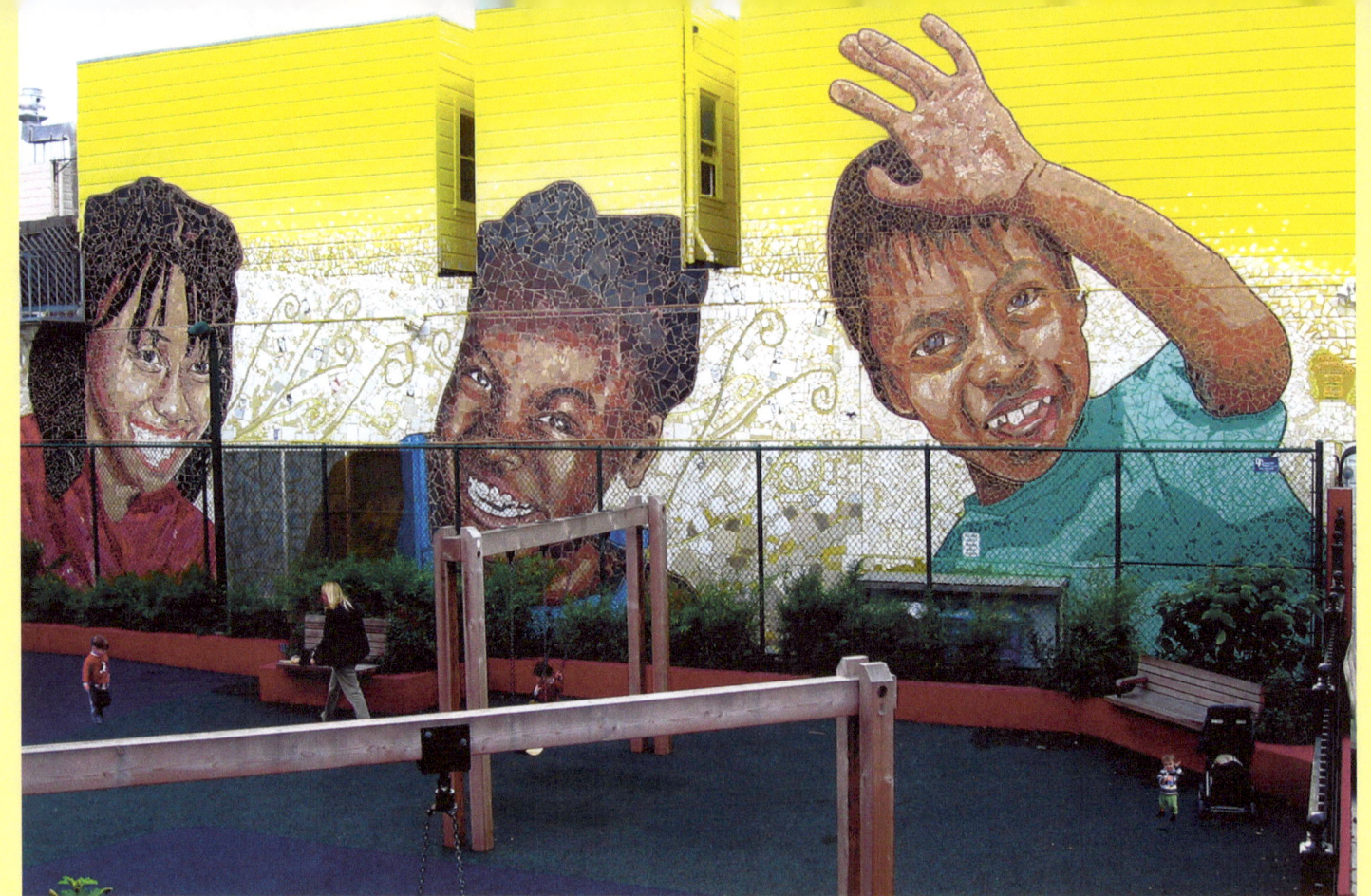

"Our Children" - The KidPower Park

The alley on Hoff Street is located near the 16th Street BART Station in San Francisco's Mission district. For decades it has been known as a throughway for drug dealers and prostitutes. In 1995 I was curating an art show at a local Taqueria and was transporting a large painting through this alley at 6:00 o'clock on a Sunday morning. As I passed a mother with her young child, I looked down and noticed that she was shooting up dope into her ankle.

There were no parks or playgrounds anywhere in this area. A few years ago a group of teenagers, with the help of their parents, began the process of converting an abandoned lot in this troubled alleyway into a safe playground where children can play.

When I contacted the owner of the building next to the new park about doing a mural, he loved the idea. During the four months of working on this mural, I got to know many of the kids and their parents in this neighborhood. My wife and two year old son Adi would come here to enjoy the playground.

There was also a lot of shouting and screaming. Drug dealing and crime was still prevalent in this alley and when it occurred, neighbors or parents would walk in to the street and confront the drug dealers, threatening to call the police. On a few occasions the drug dealers would do business in the playground itself. The residents of the alley were militant in their efforts to protect this space.

I chose to do three large portraits of children, because I feel that the needs of children in this neighborhood have often been overlooked. The mural was intended to celebrate not only the children playing in this park, but the community activism that was behind reclaiming this urban space.

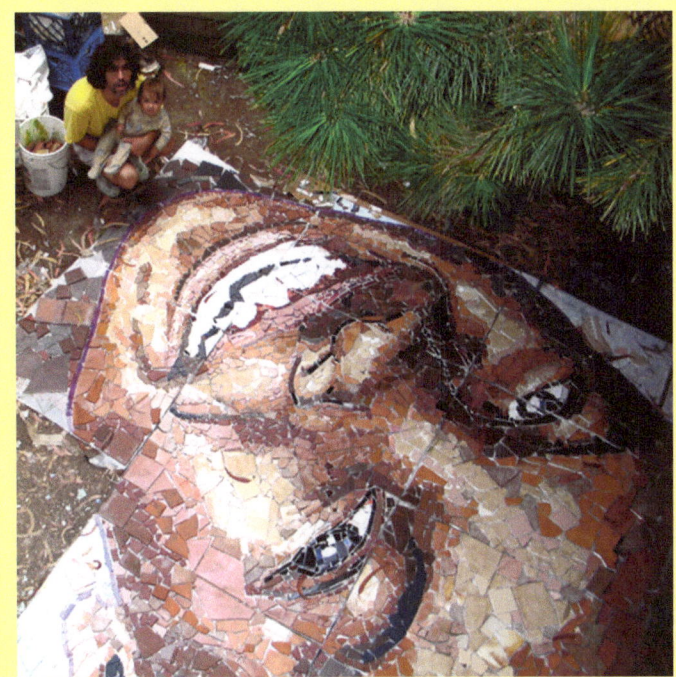

The faces were created on nylon mesh and assembled on the wall like a giant jigsaw puzzle.

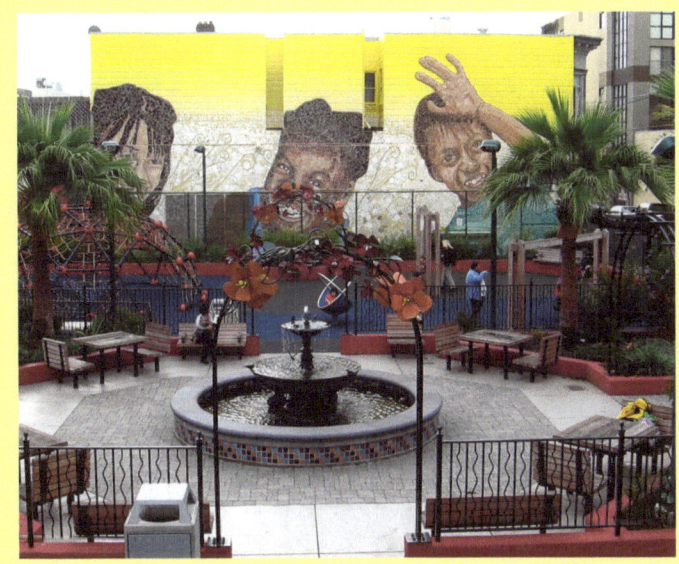

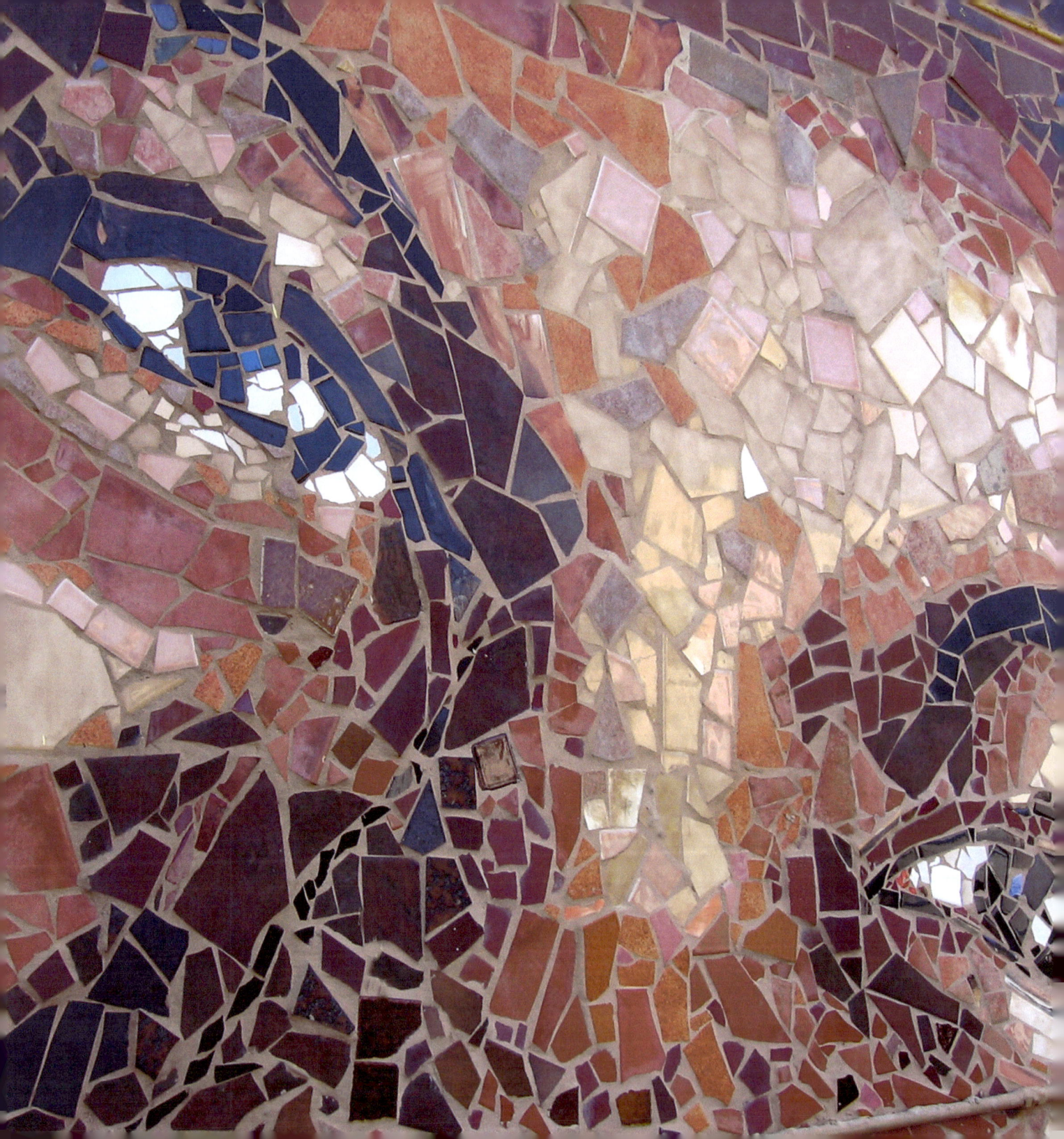

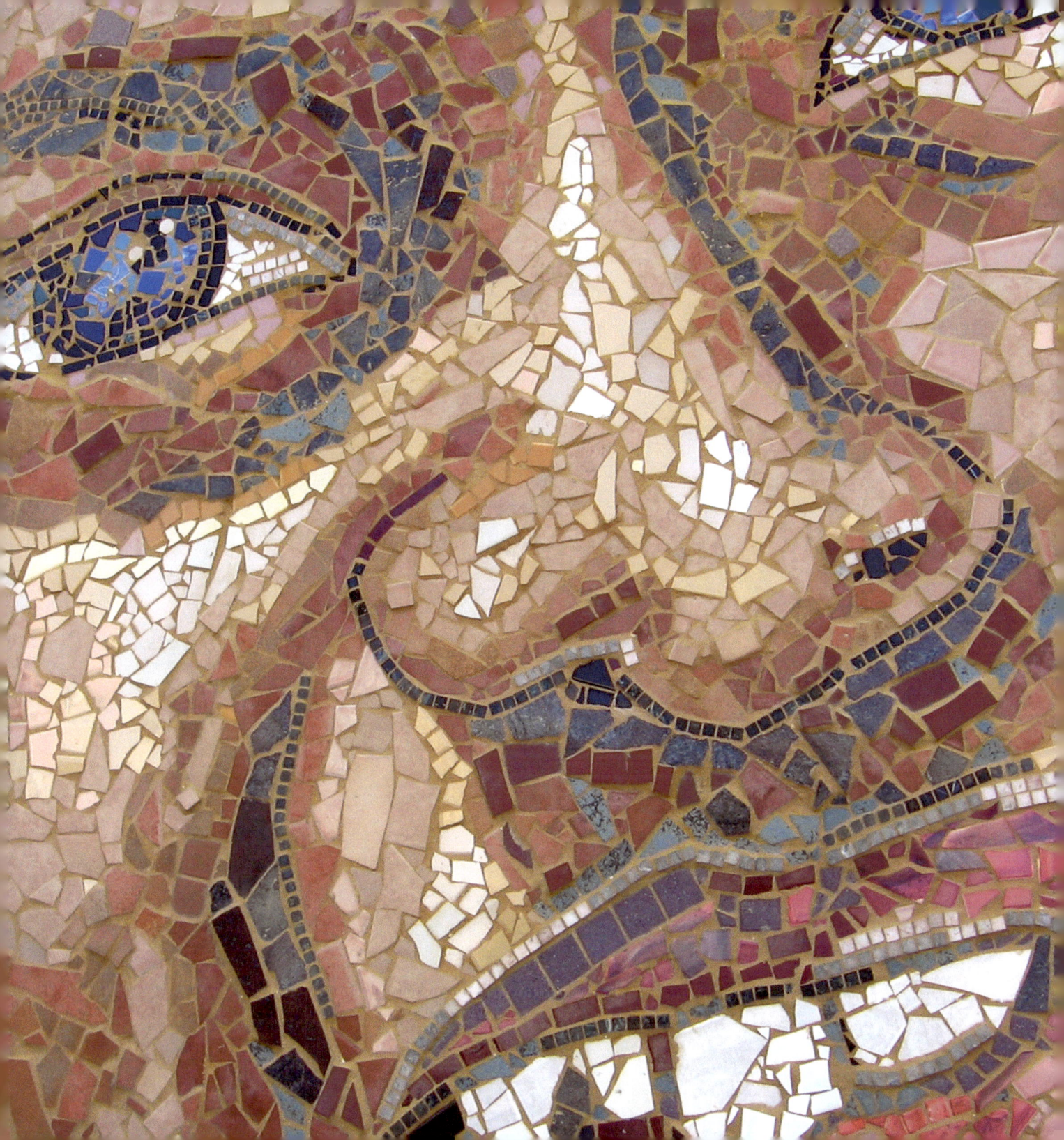

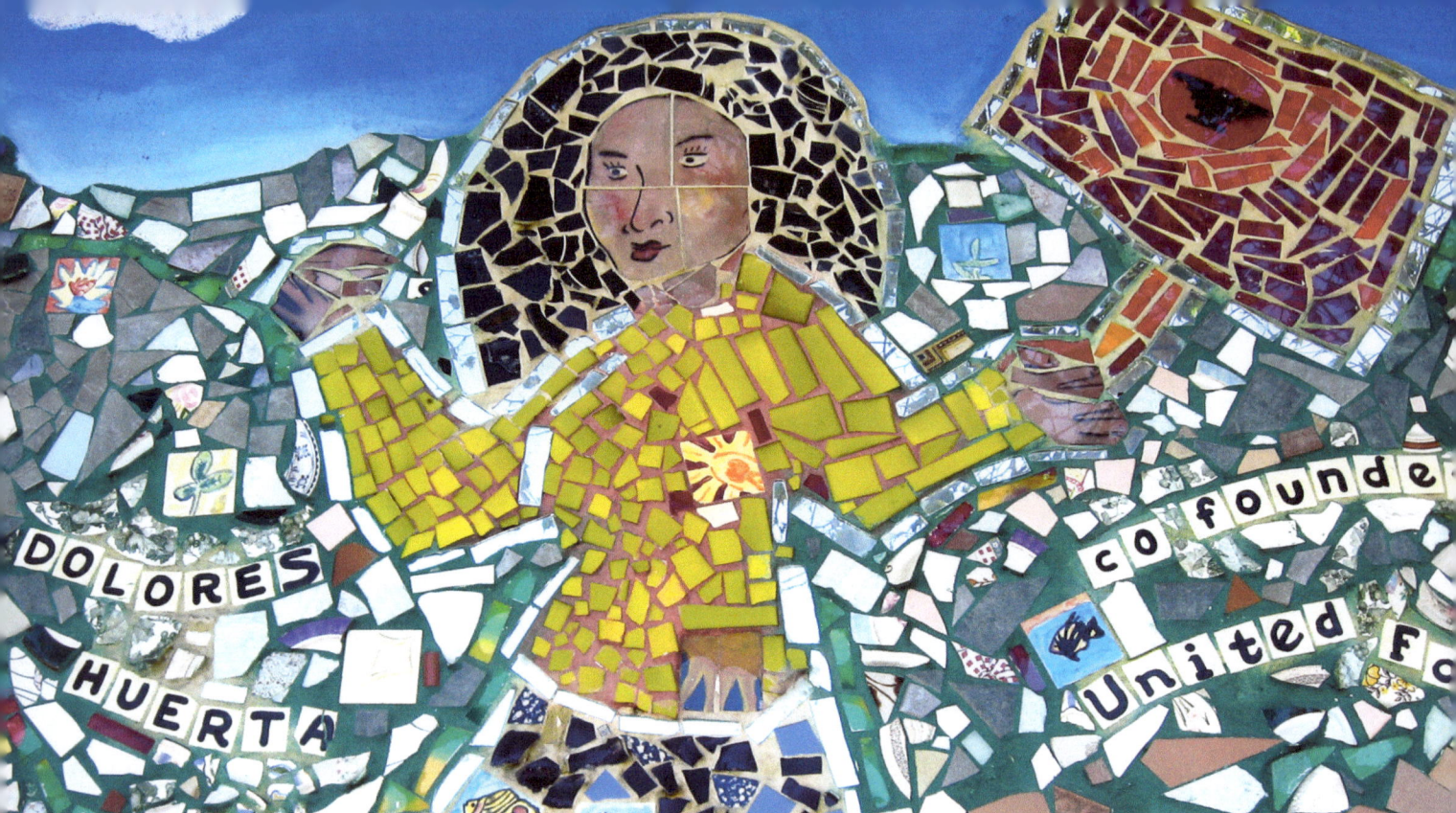

A Tribute to Dolores Huerta

For this project I partnered with a 5th grade teacher at Leonard R. Flynn Elementary School in the Mission district. This was a class where all of the kids were Spanish speaking and learning English. As part of teaching 5th grade California labor history, the students were learning about the life of Dolores Huerta, co-founder of the United Farm Workers.

One of Ms. Huerta's daughters, Camilla Chavez, was living in the area and agreed to meet with the kids while they were researching their mural. She talked about being a child growing up in a family of union organizers and that many migrant workers' children still work in the fields in Salinas. She asked them who their heroes were. The students raised their hands and said: "Cesar Chavez, Martin Luther King, Gandhi".

"Those are great heroes," Camilla told the class, "but nobody mentioned any women. Children in this neighborhood will grow up knowing who Dolores Huerta is because of the mural you kids are making. This is really important!"

After the design was approved, the students spent 6 weeks working on scaffolding on the outside of their school, creating their mosaic mural. The school faces Cesar Chavez Boulevard (a major street in the city), where many day laborers solicit work from passing trucks.

For the mural unveiling, Dolores Huerta herself came up from Bakersfield to speak to the school and to the young artists.

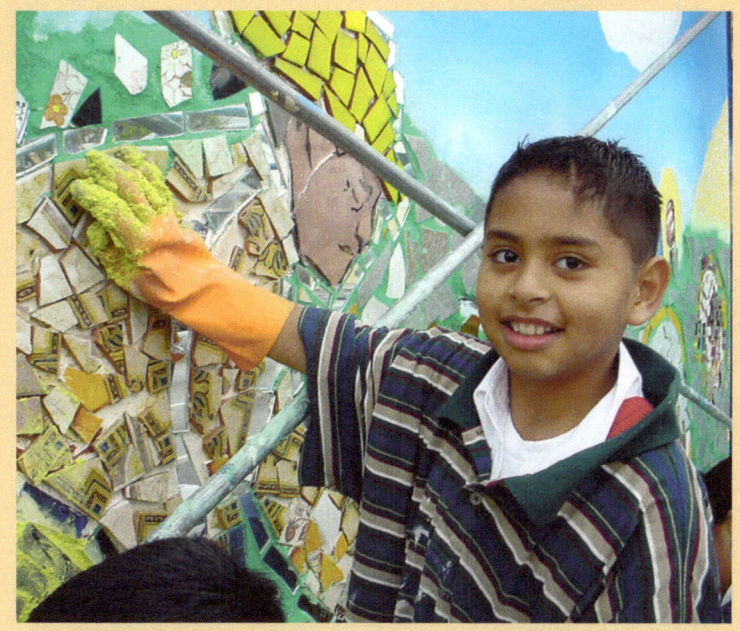

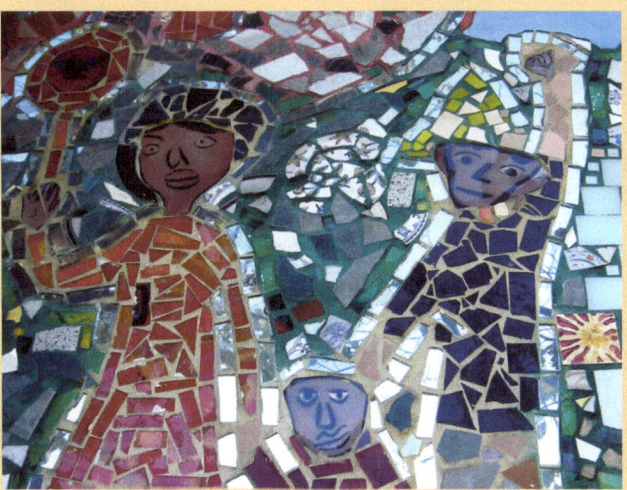

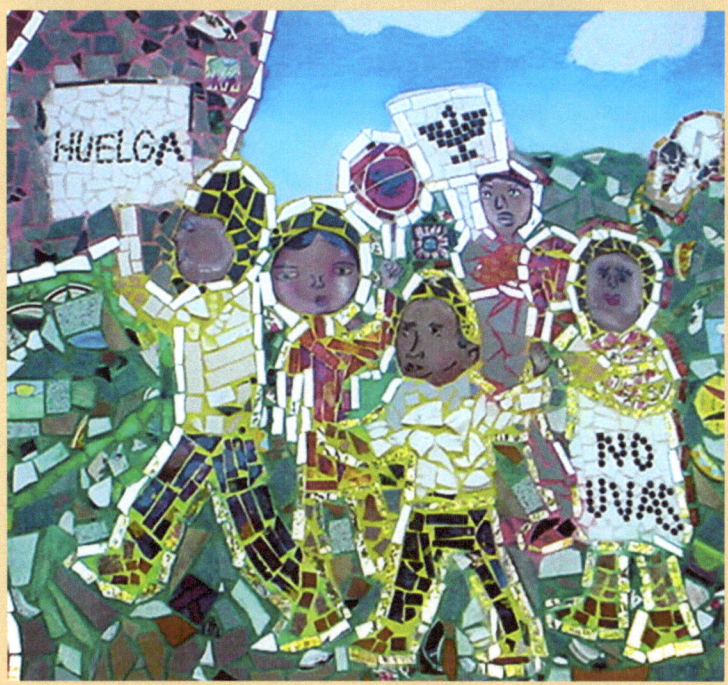

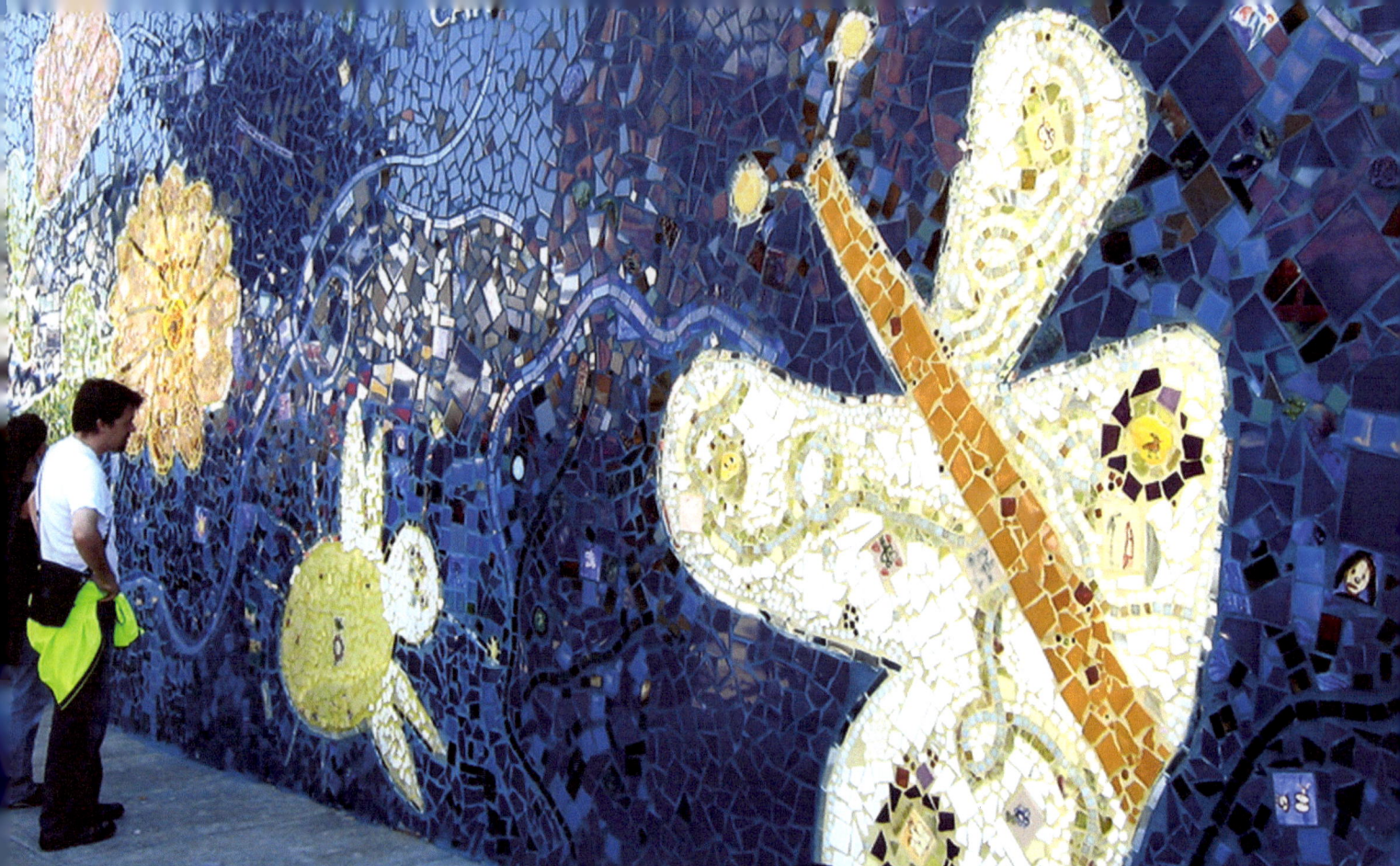

The Children's Village Mural

In the Spring of 2006 I was approached by a pre-school located in San Francisco's South of Market (SOMA) district. Like many inner-city schools, the area around this school has a lot of problems with crime, drugs and prostitution. It is not uncommon to see homeless camps on the steps of the church right next to this pre-school. At the entrance of the school was a 13' high x 40' wide cement wall that had been plagued by graffiti for years.

The goal with this mural was to beautify this wall and show the thousands of cars driving past every day that young children were beginning their education in this building.

Over a six-week period, I met with a class of 4 years olds to create tiles and ceramic pieces. I had never worked with children this young before.

With the help of adult supervision the 4 year olds did a great job of laying tile and grouting. Many did better than the middle school students I work with. We tried involving some 3 year olds and found that they were just too young.

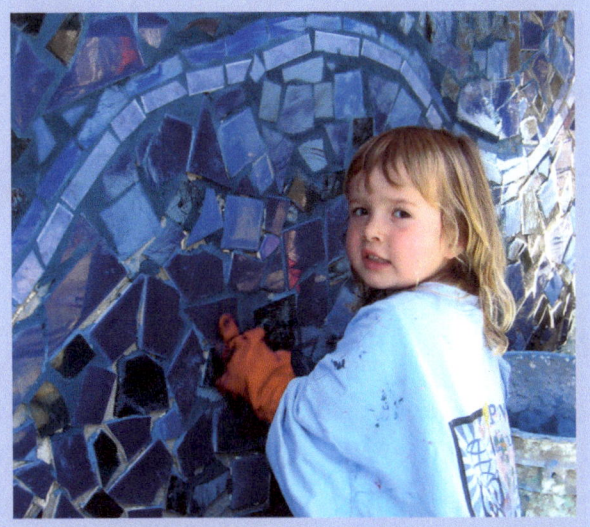

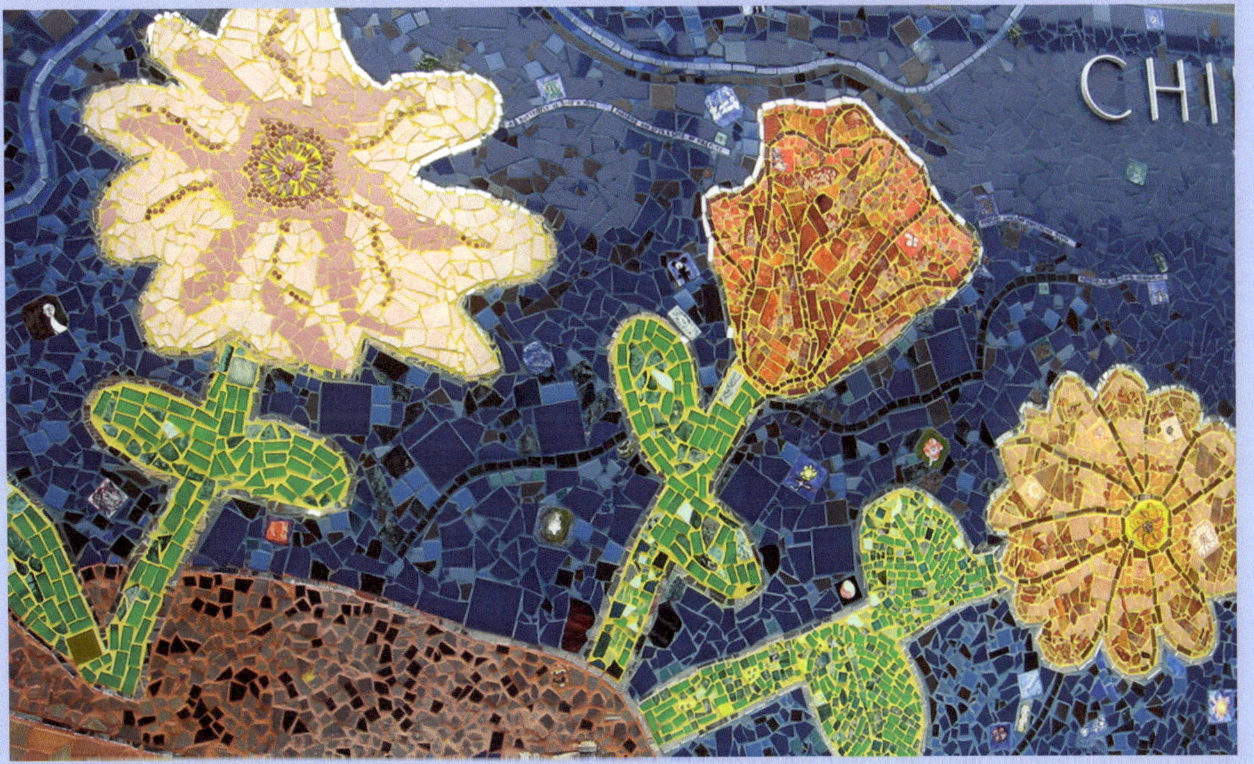

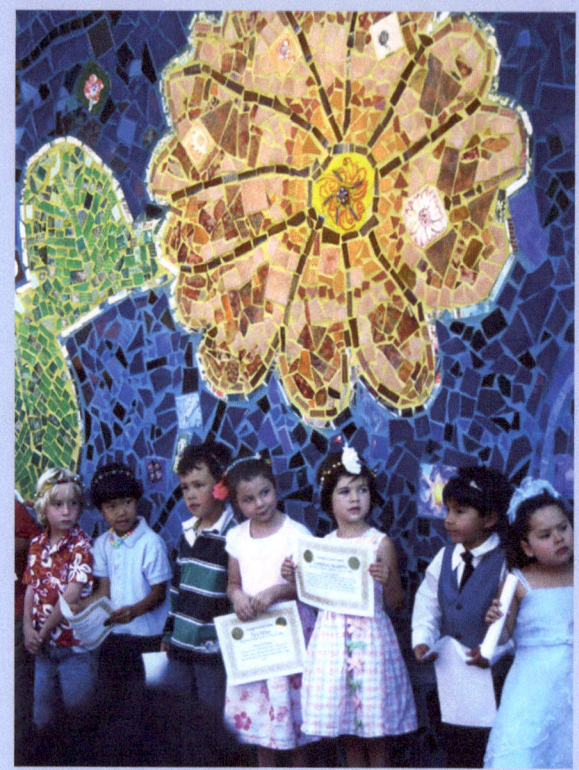

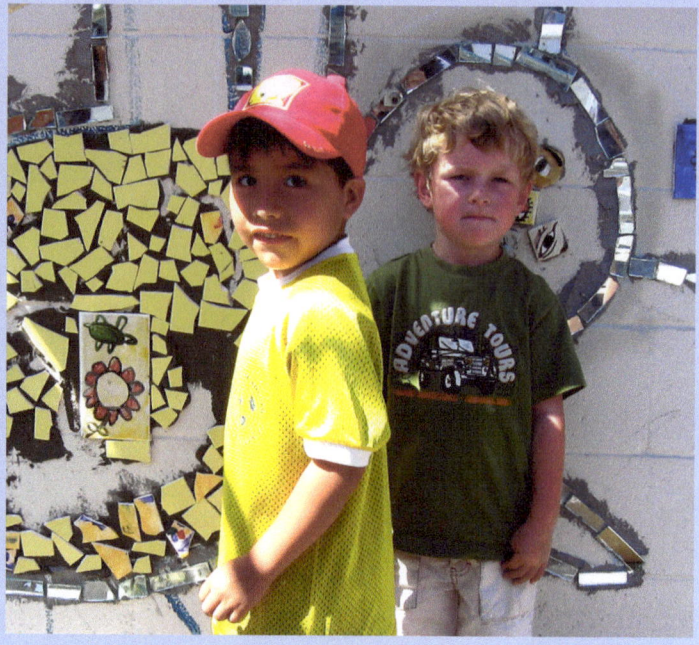

The mural unveiling was incorporated into the graduation ceremony.

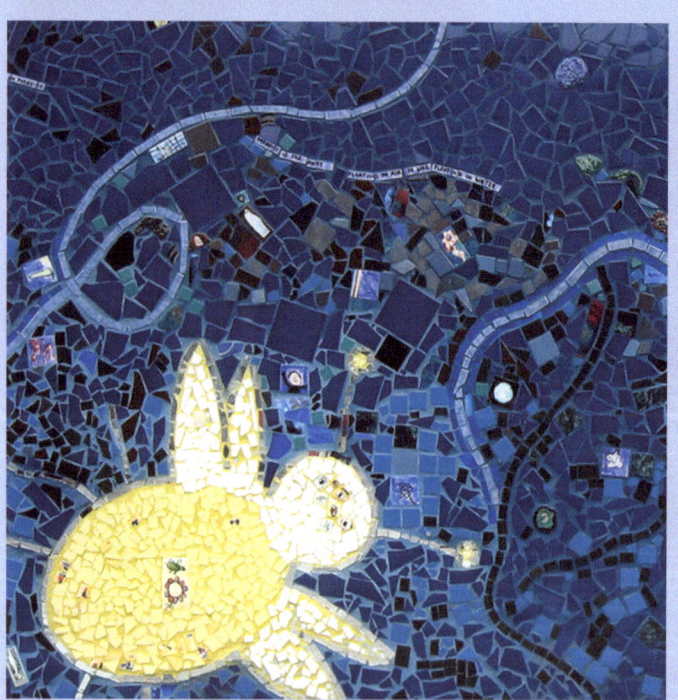

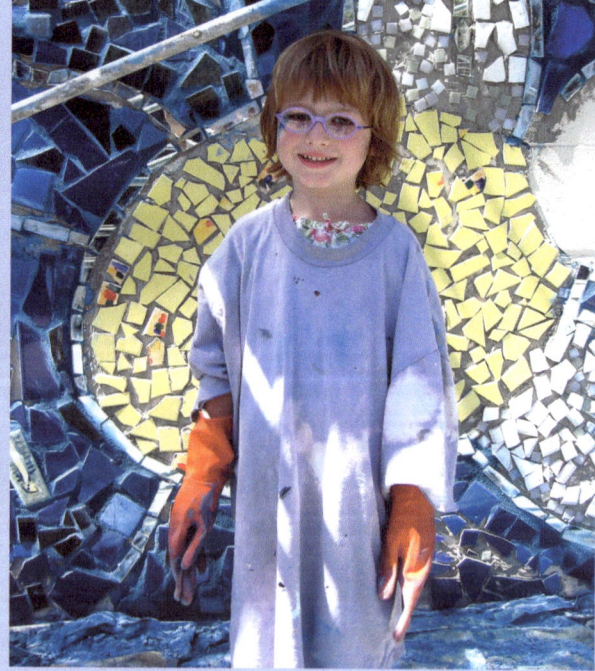

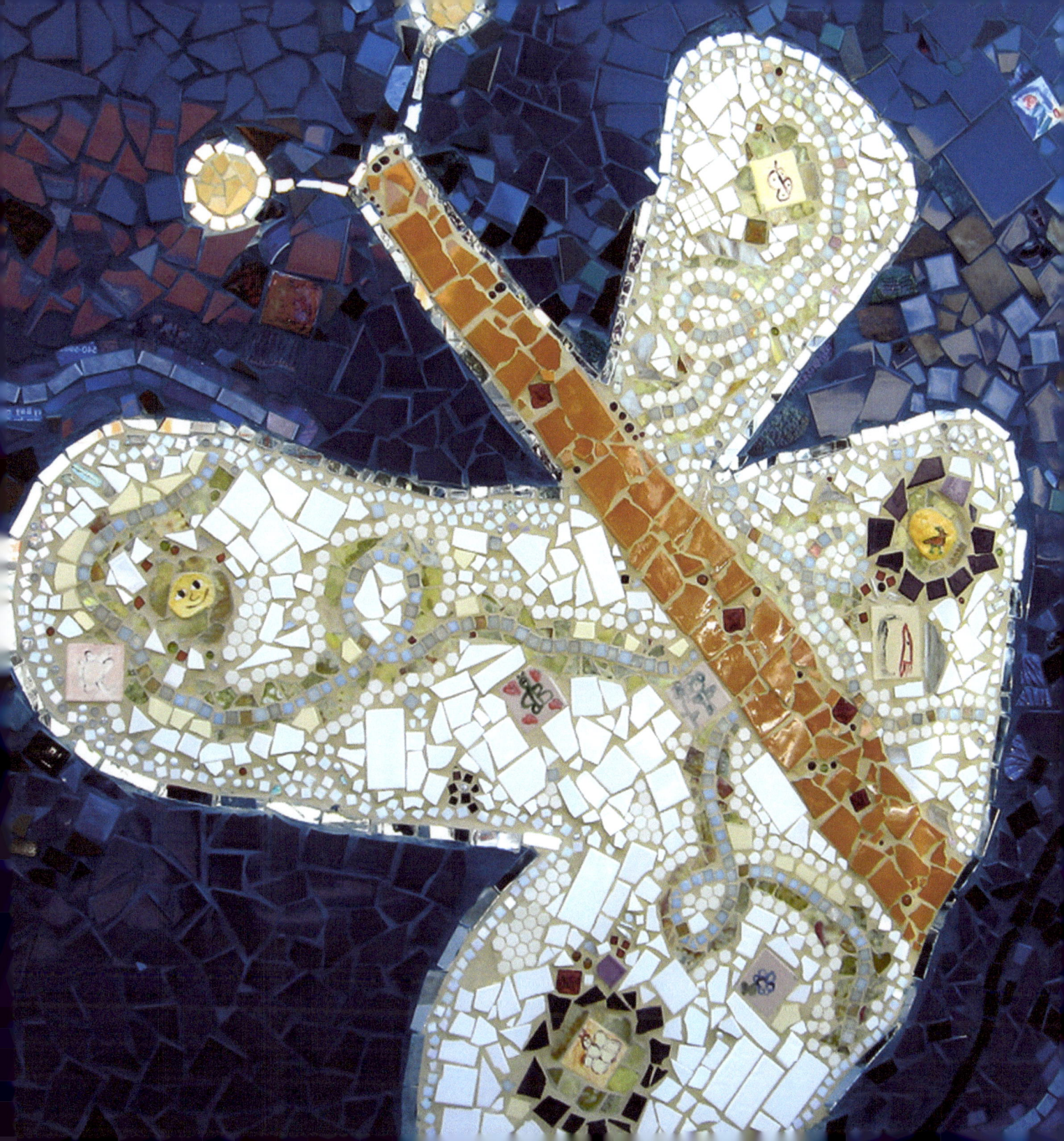

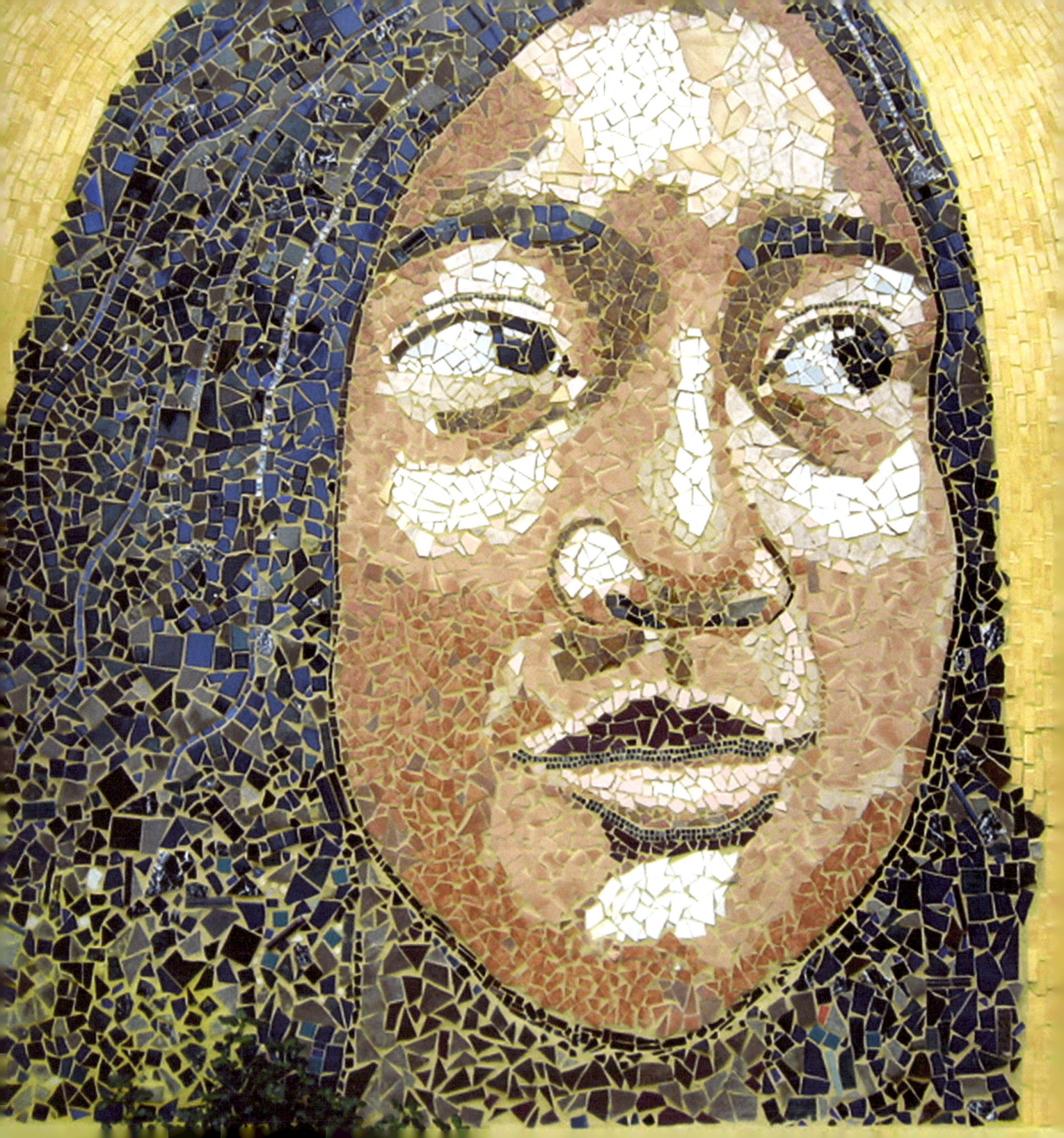

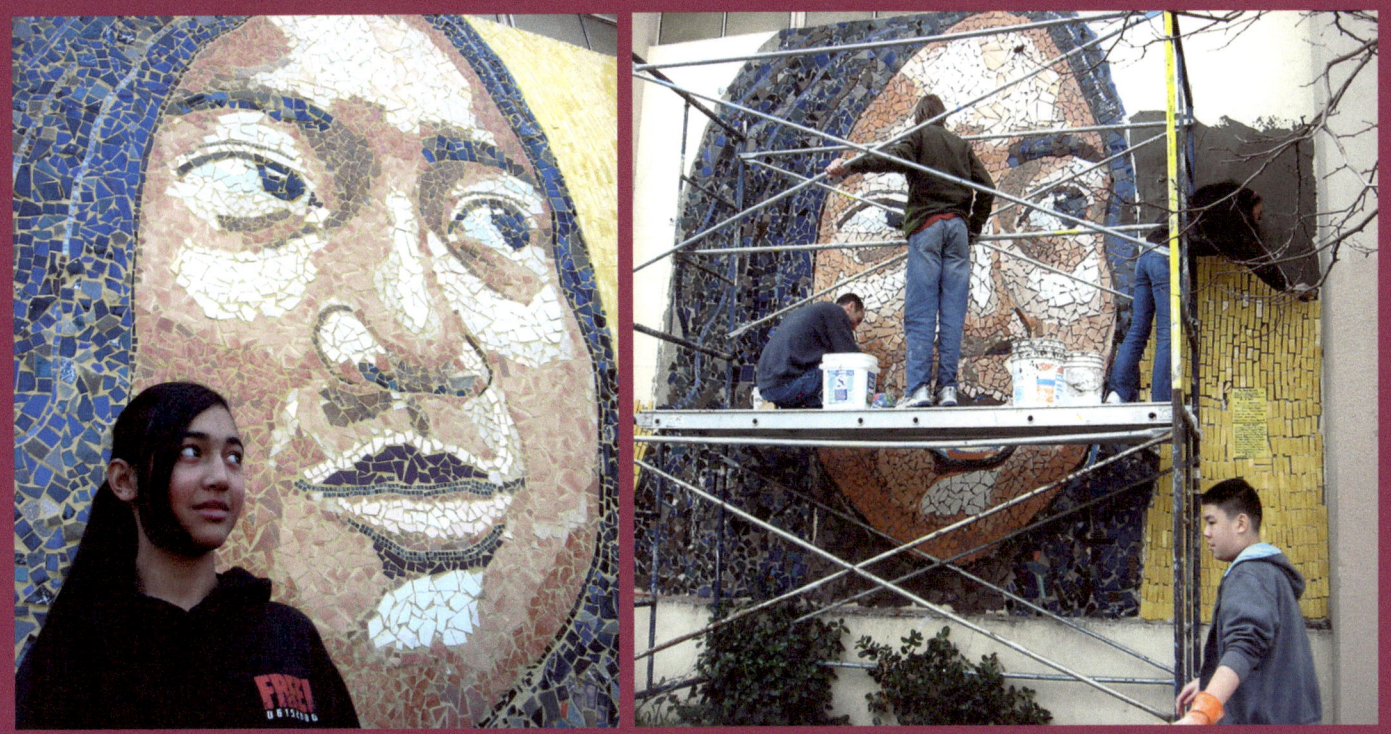

The Urban Portrait Project

I got the idea for this project several years ago while walking around the streets of Philadelphia. There was a series of outdoor tile portraits created by artist Mary DeWitt, featuring women on Pennsylvania's death row. Before seeing these murals it never occurred to me that there *were* women on death row. I started to think about ignored people in America, and how many of our inner-city school children have joined the ranks of people like the homeless and incarcerated who are an increasingly invisible population in our cities.

The Urban Portrait Project is an on-going series of portraits featuring school children in inner city schools. Over the next 10 years, I hope to have 50 mosaic portraits around the Bay Area. Some of the portraits will be Josef Norris murals; some will be created by young people.

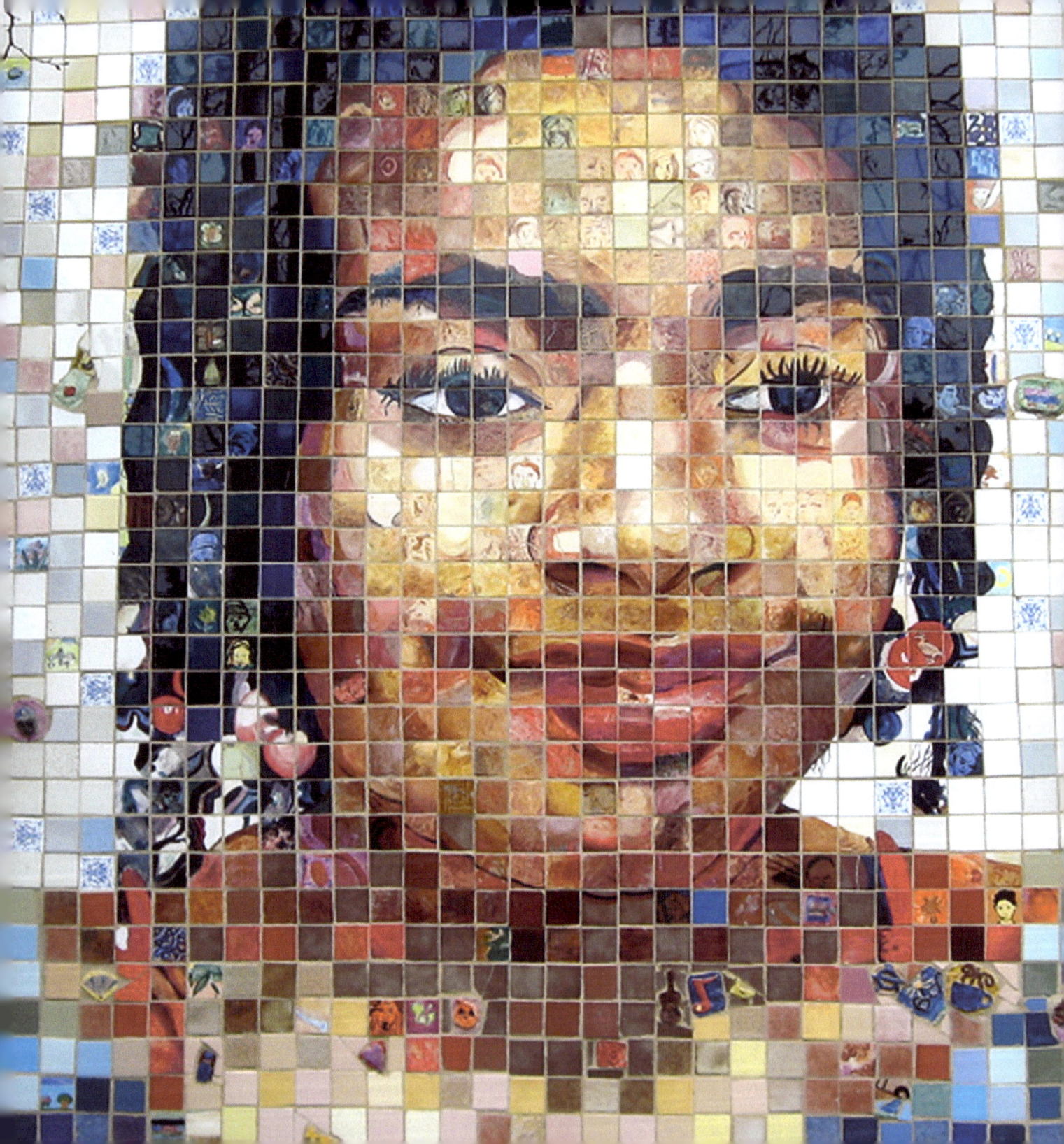

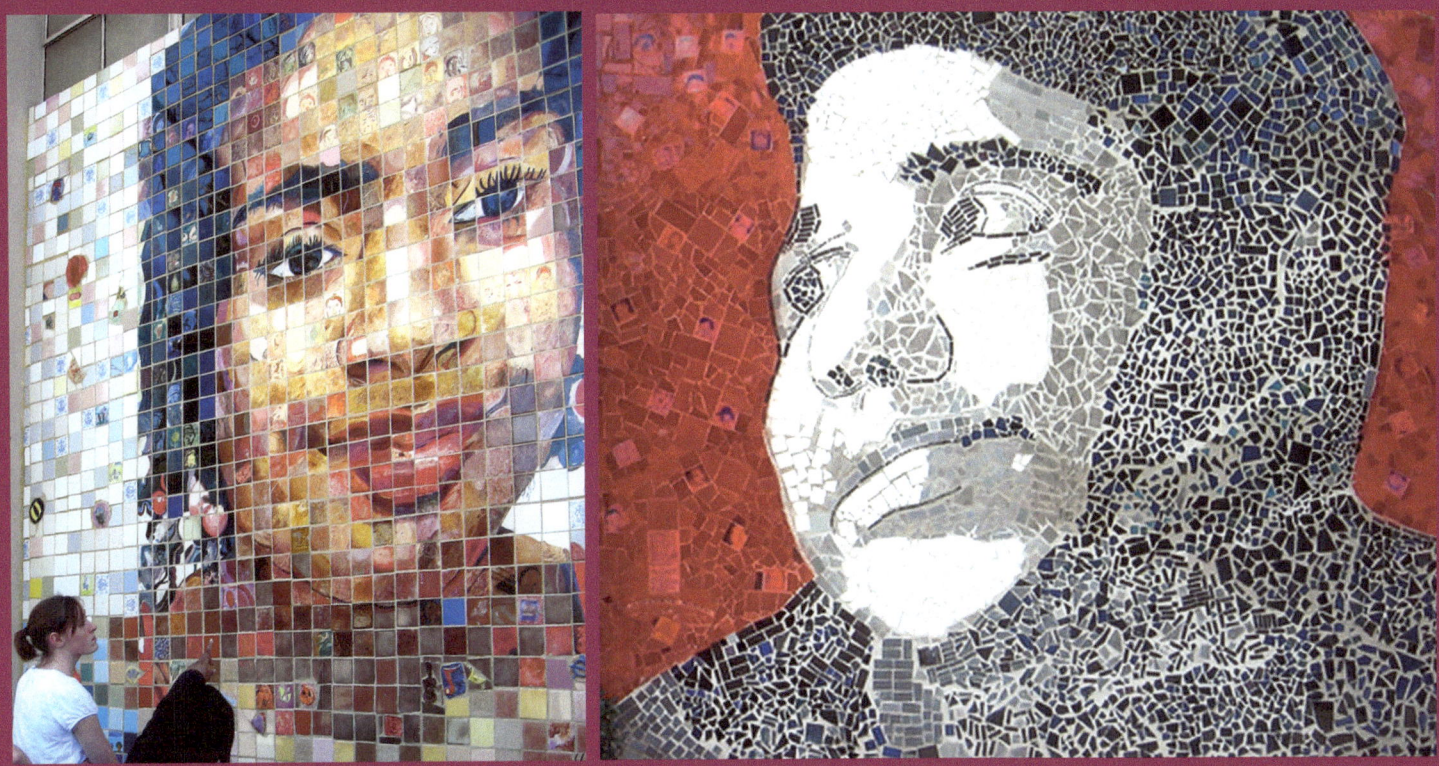

For the first four portraits, a class of 8th graders at KIPP San Francisco Bay Academy and a class of 9th graders at Gateway Charter High School created four large-scale mosaic portraits on the outside of their Western Addition School on a wall facing Geary Boulevard. Each portrait measured 14' high x 14' wide and is seen by thousands of commuters every day.

Students studied different types of portraiture including the large grid paintings of Chuck Close. They watched the video "Maya Lin - A Clear Vision" about her struggles creating the controversial Vietnam War Memorial at age 20. The students then did a photo-shoot, creating portraits of eachother. In a heated classroom debate the students voted on which portraits to use. During the last 6 weeks, 28 students in each class worked in shifts on scaffolding to create their murals.

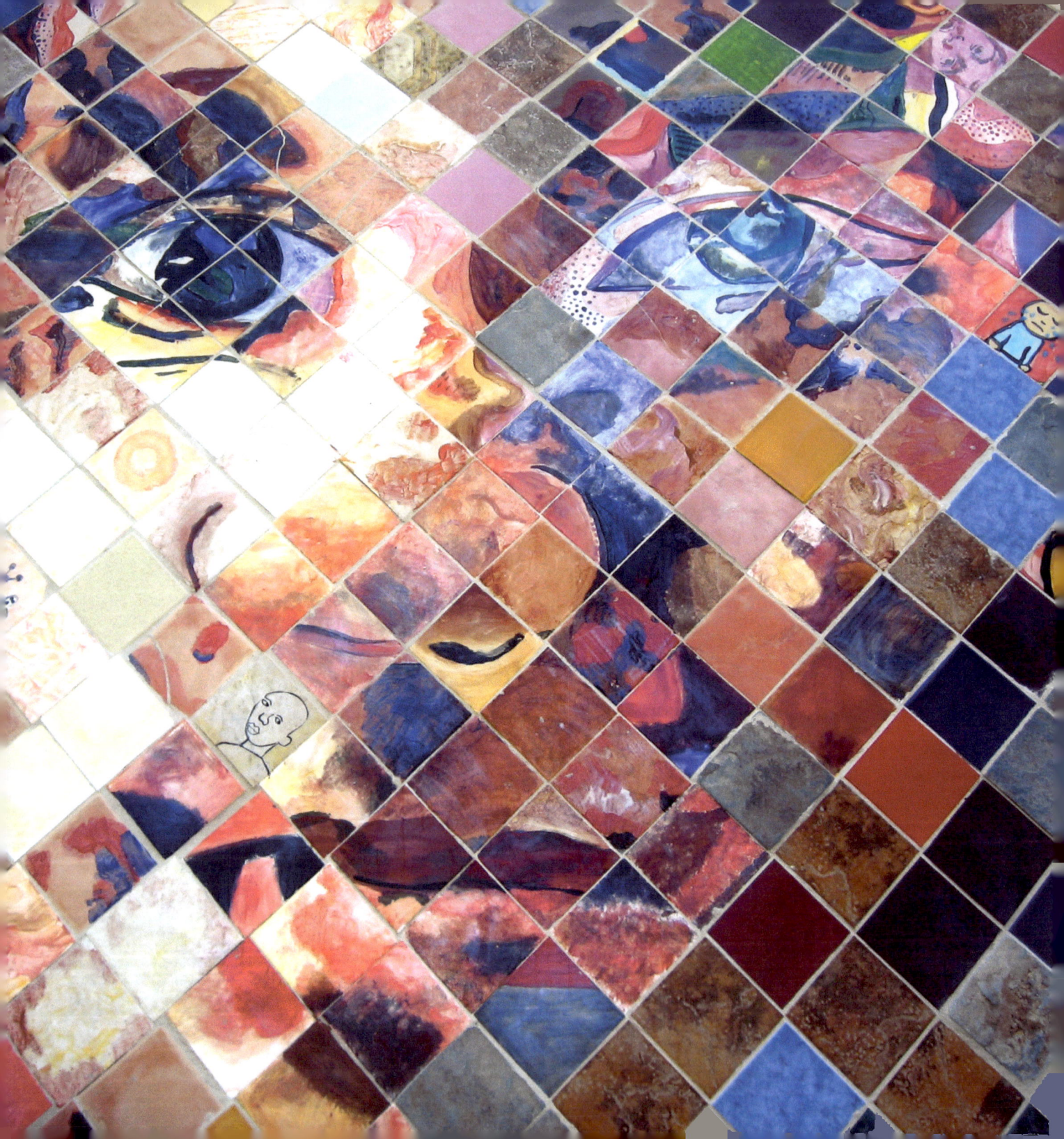

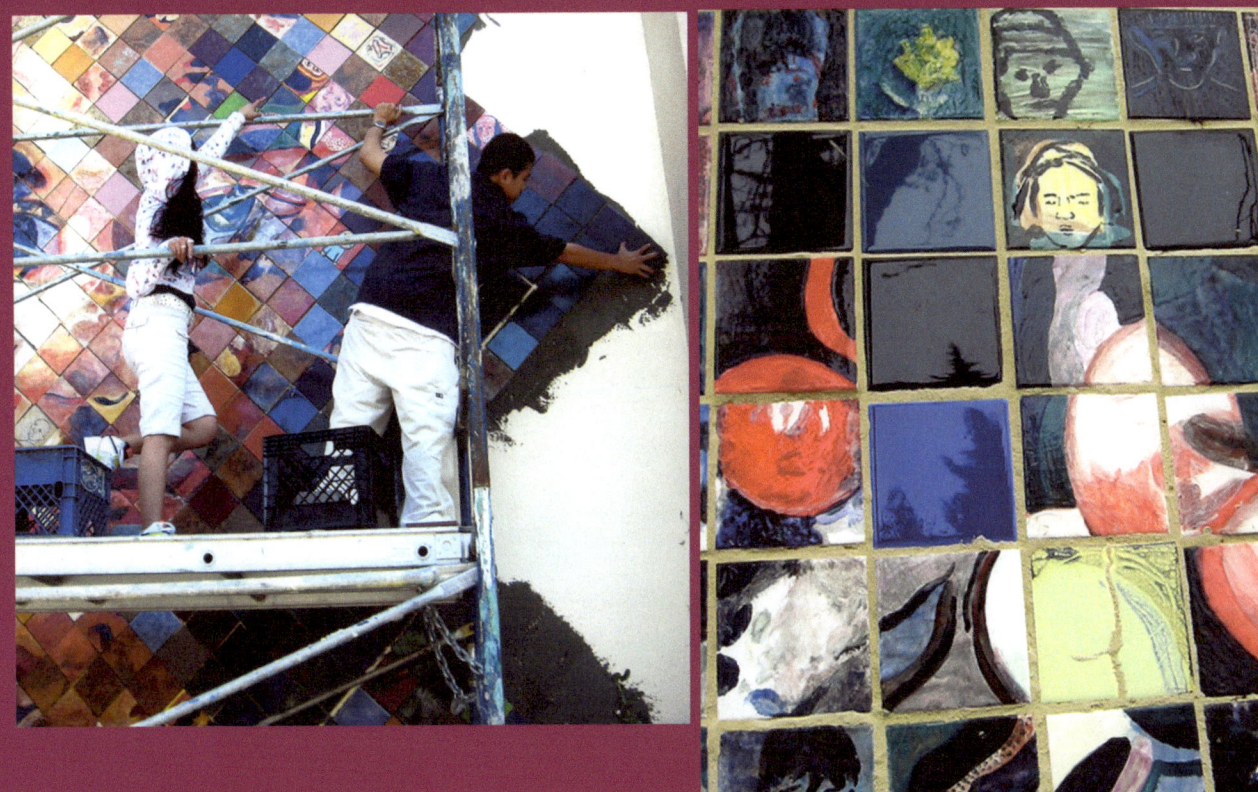

Grid Portraits

Two of the portraits were modeled after the Chuck Close grid paintings. We took the two chosen photographs, made a very large print-out, and cut them into 1,200 and 800 pieces. The students then blindly recreated each cut out square onto a bisque tile that was then glazed and fired in a kiln. We also chose scores of solid colors and tiles from salvage yards to make up the rest of the portrait. After carefully numbering the tiles and storing them in crates, we assembled each grid portrait on to the masonry, building it like a brick wall.

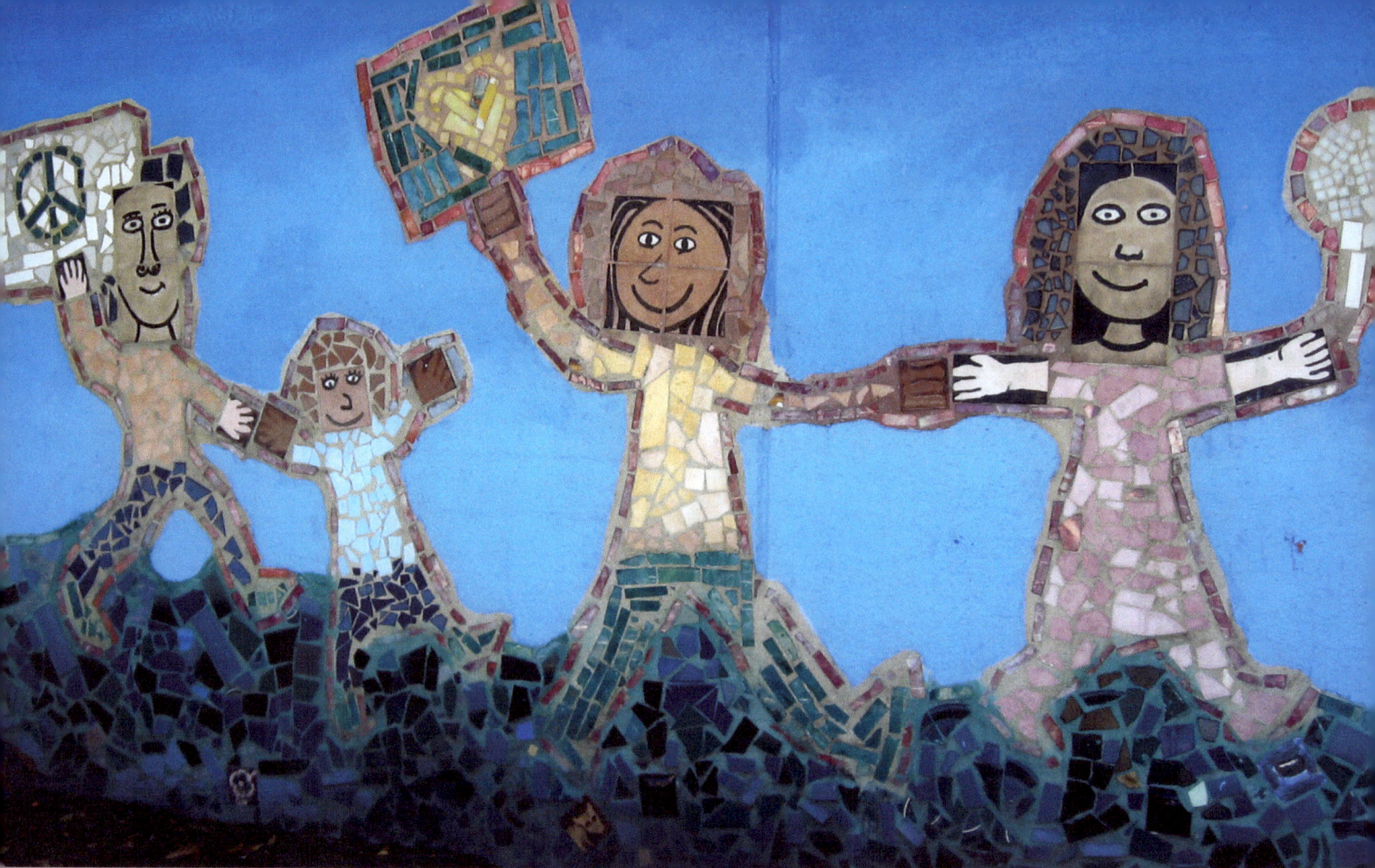

The Community Peace Mural

Bret Harte Elementary School is located in the backyard of Candlestick Park in San Francisco's Bayview Hunters Point district. When I approached principal Vidrale Franklin, she immediately said she wanted the mural's theme to be about making peace. Not just that peace is a good thing - she wanted the students to explore how communities come together to create peace. The school is located directly across the street from two housing projects, and there had been drive-by shootings recently that shook up the neighborhood.

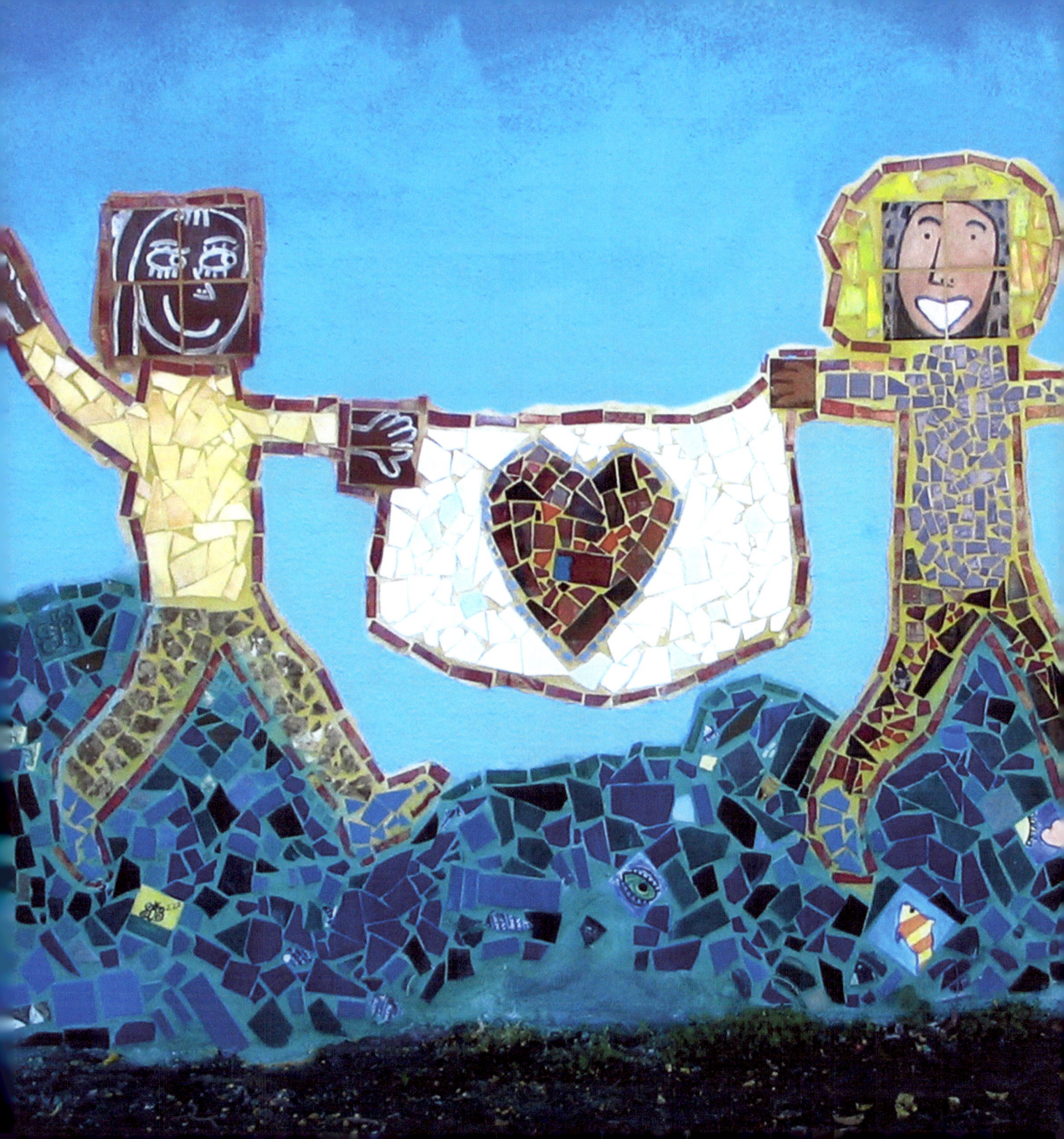

Working with two 3rd grade teachers, the students developed a series of questions. The teachers invited people from the neighborhood to come to class and be interviewed by the kids. One of the invited guests was singer Michael Franti, from the band Spearhead, who lives in Bayview Hunters Point. He had just come back from a trip to Iraq and talked about visiting soldiers and wounded children in this war-torn country. He brought his guitar and guided the kids through some of his songs like: "Everyone Deserves Music" and "Power to the Peaceful". When asked how a community makes peace - he said "It is really important for you to get to know your neighbors!"

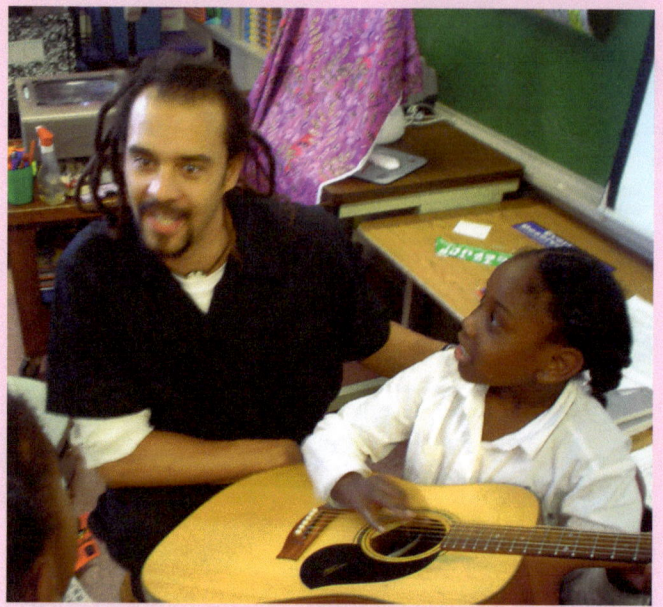

Michael Franti with the 3rd grade artists

Ms. Franklin, the school principal, was also interviewed by the students. She grew up in the neighborhood and also spoke of the need for getting to know your neighbors. One of the 3rd grade classes was predominantly African-American. The second participating class was entirely Latino (with many kids learning English as a second language).

She talked about how at recess the two classes do not play with each other but stay in their own groups. She created an assignment where the students from each class had to interview a student in the other class and then write a

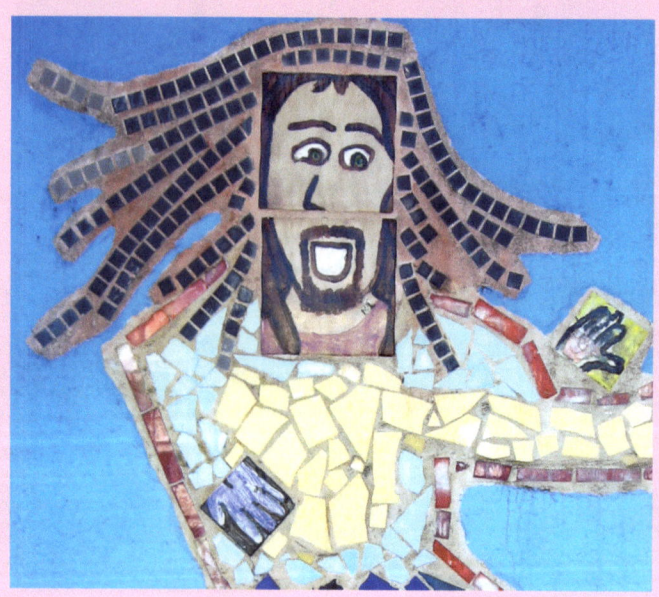

...and on the finished mural

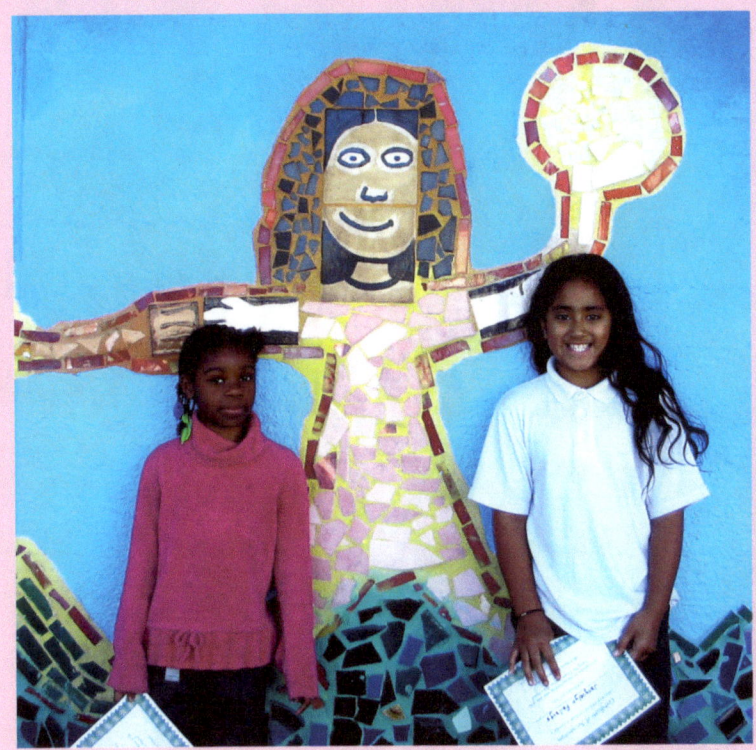
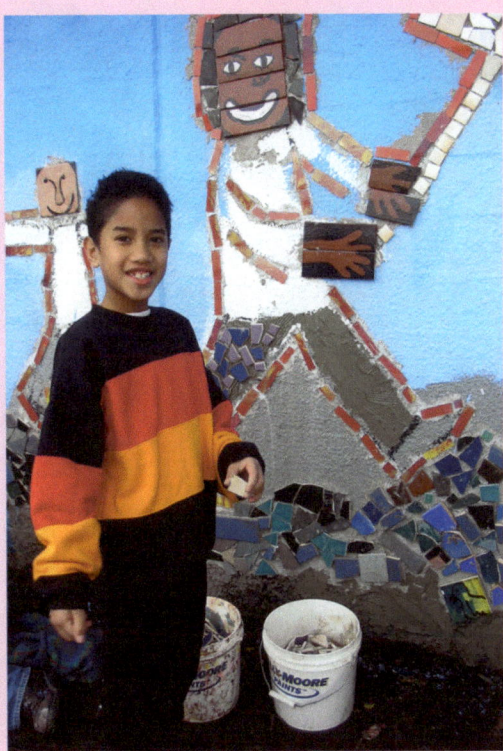

report about what they had learned about that person.

During the first 5 weeks of this design process, I learned that during Martin Luther King's Birthday the school gets a police escort and holds a peace march through the housing project across the street. I asked the students to draw pictures of what the march was like. These drawings became the basis for the mural design.

Each morning, while getting the 70' wide mural wall ready for the students, I would watch the entire school gather in the yard to begin their day. Instead of the usual pledging allegiance to the flag - the principal, megaphone in hand, would lead the students in a chorus of "We Shall Overcome". It became very clear that this mural was part of a much larger effort on the part of this community.

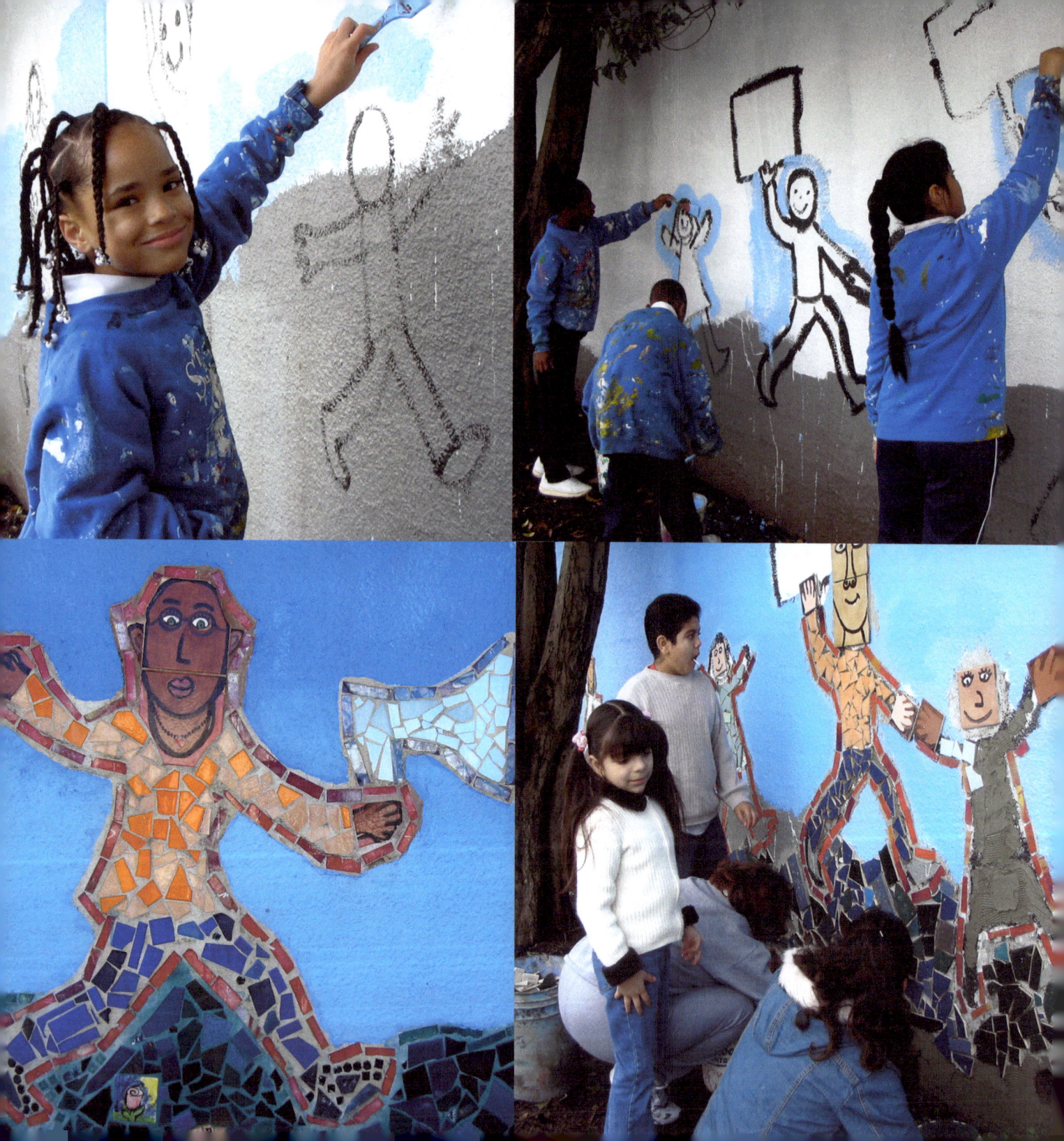

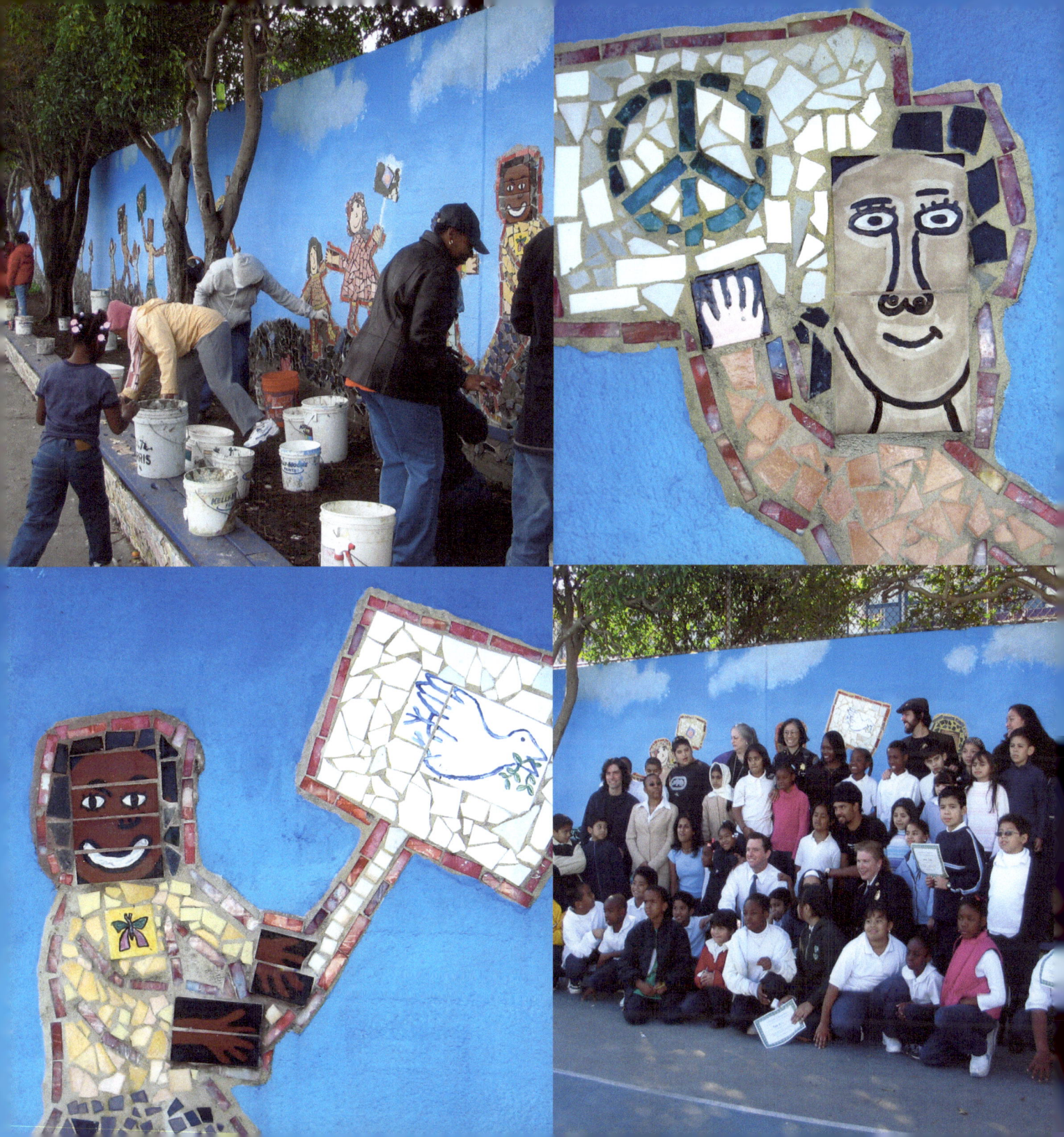

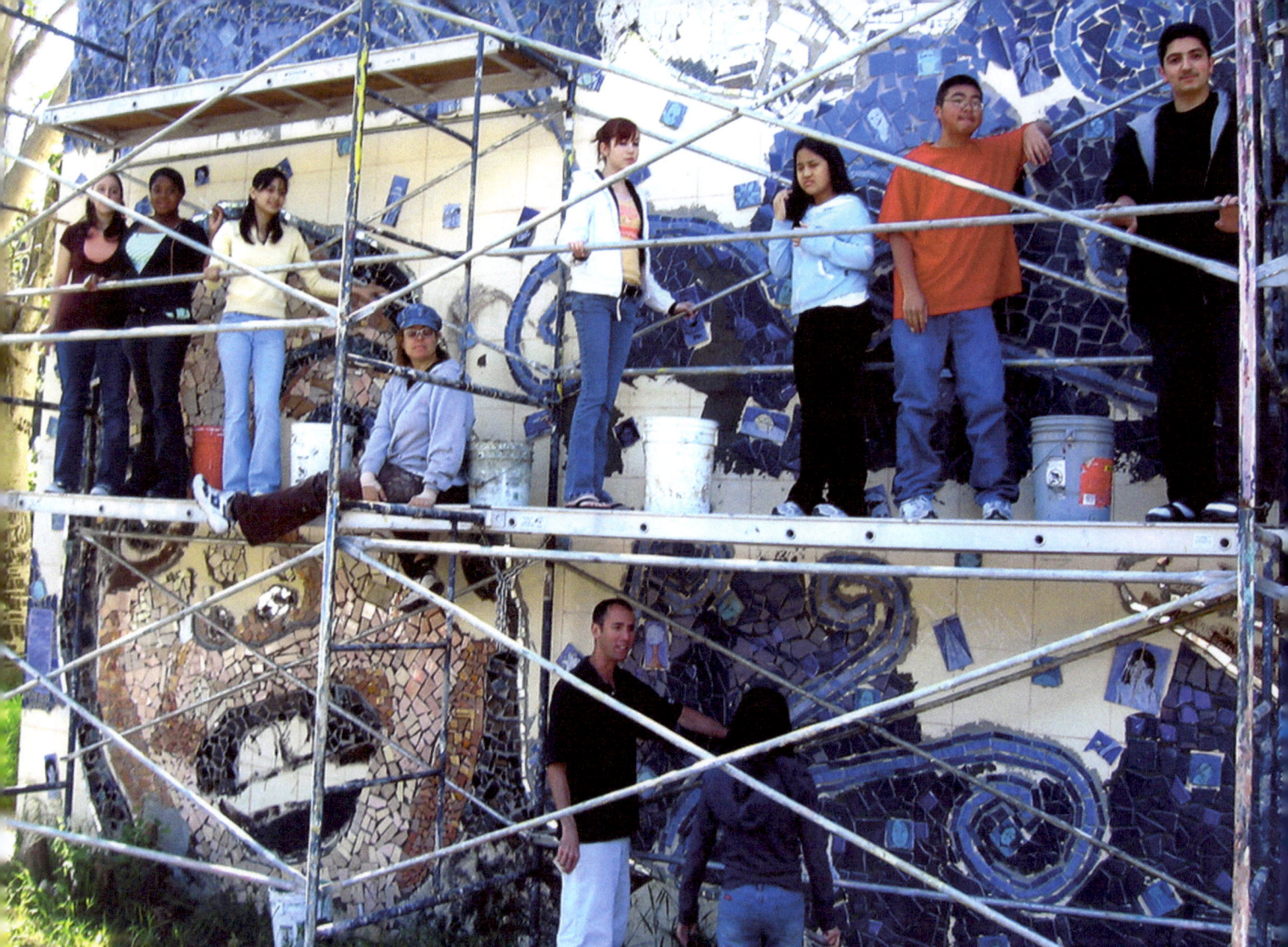

Hope

This mural was created as part of a 9th grade class at Gateway Charter High School. The semester began with a teenager being shot and killed near the front steps of the high school. During the first 6 weeks of the project, students did art projects and writing about the nature of violence - in our neighborhood, our city and our world.

Mosaics provide many opportunities for young people to have ownership in their murals. For this project students created stencils of people and painted tiles that were fired in a kiln and incorporated into the mural.

For one assignment, students were asked to paint an image on a tile that defined their generation.

On the far right side of the picture you can see an image of a plane flying into the twin towers.

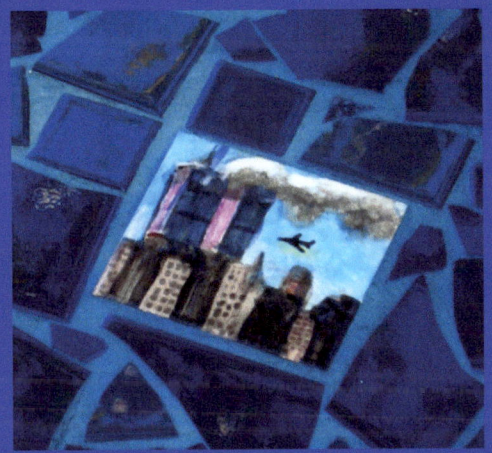

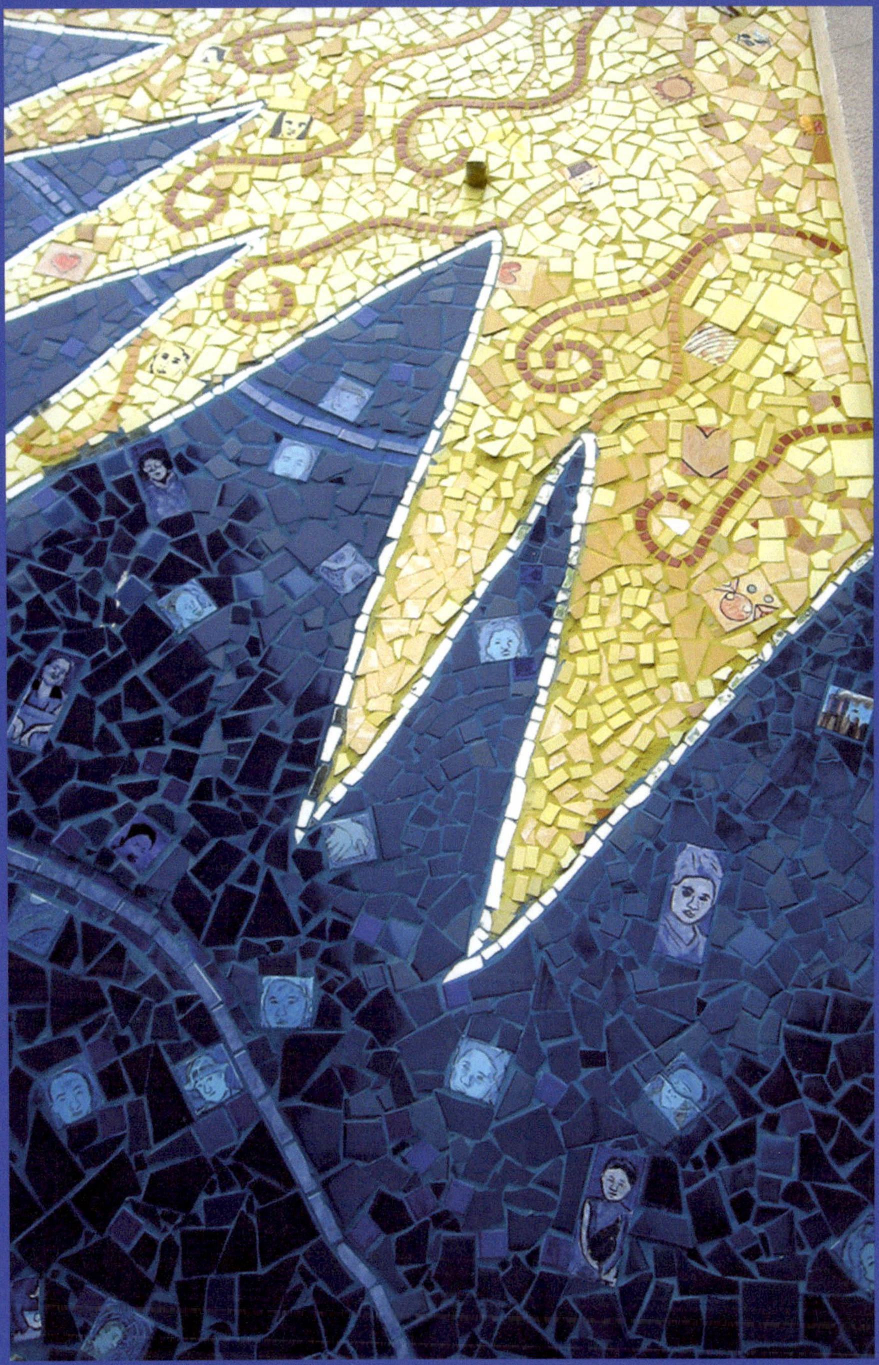

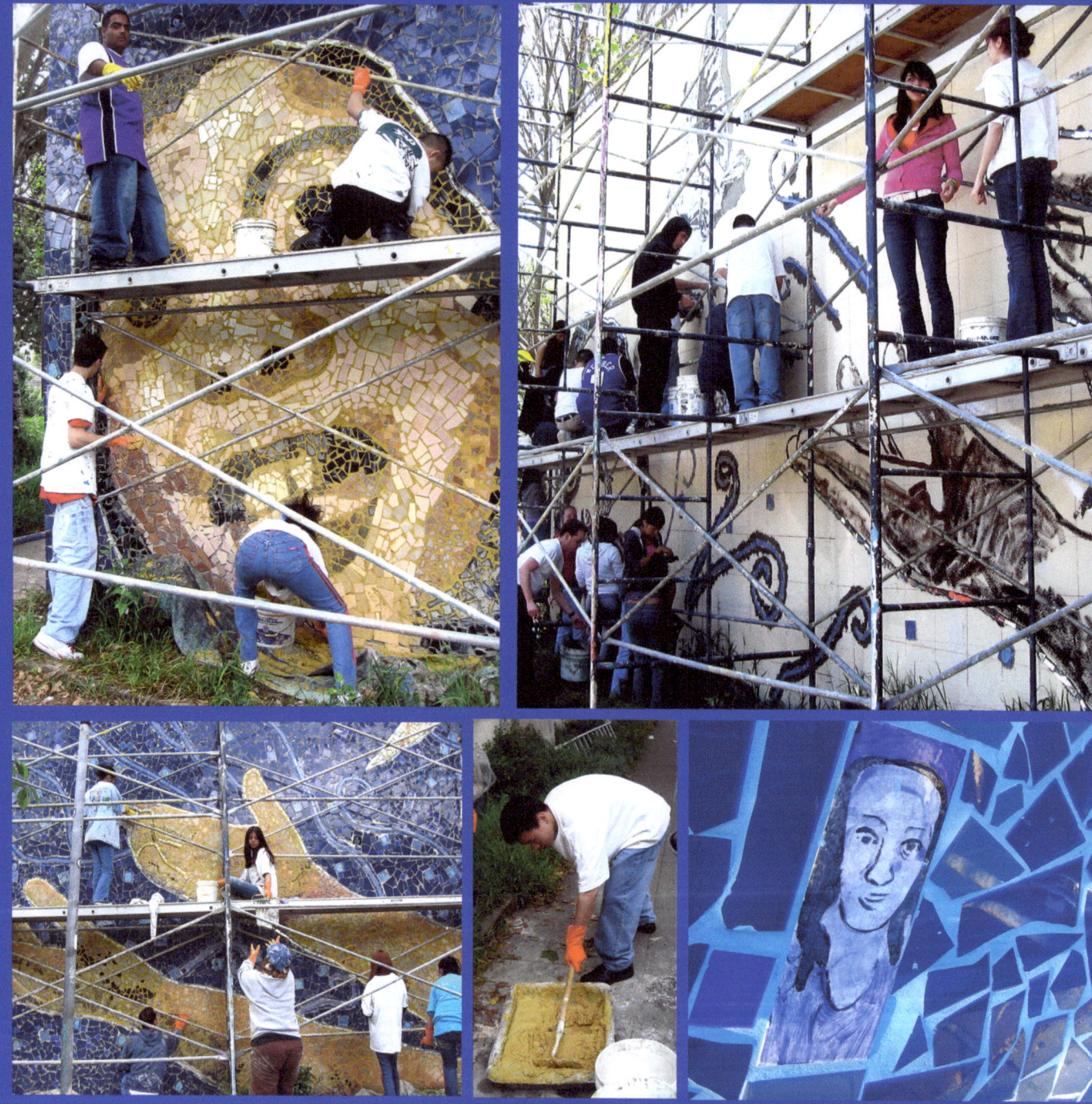

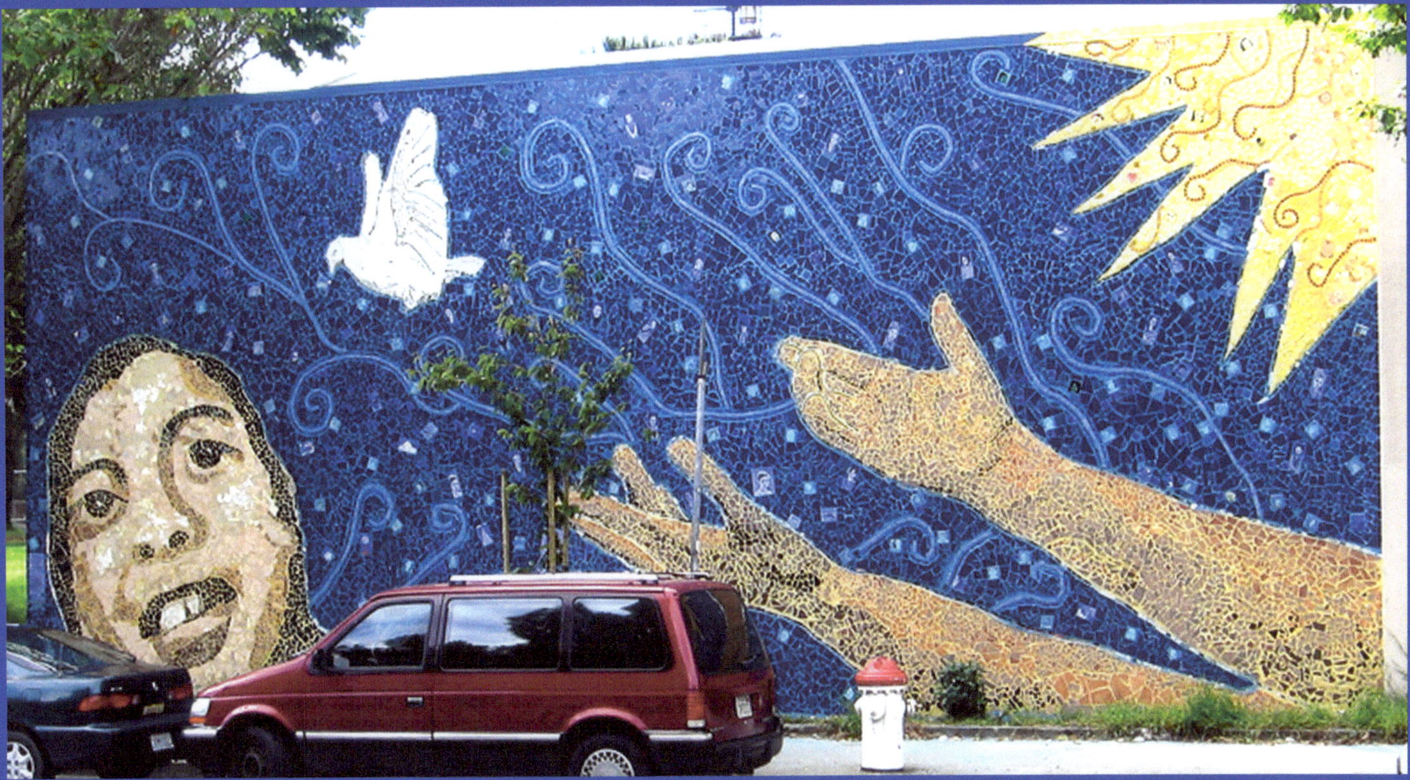

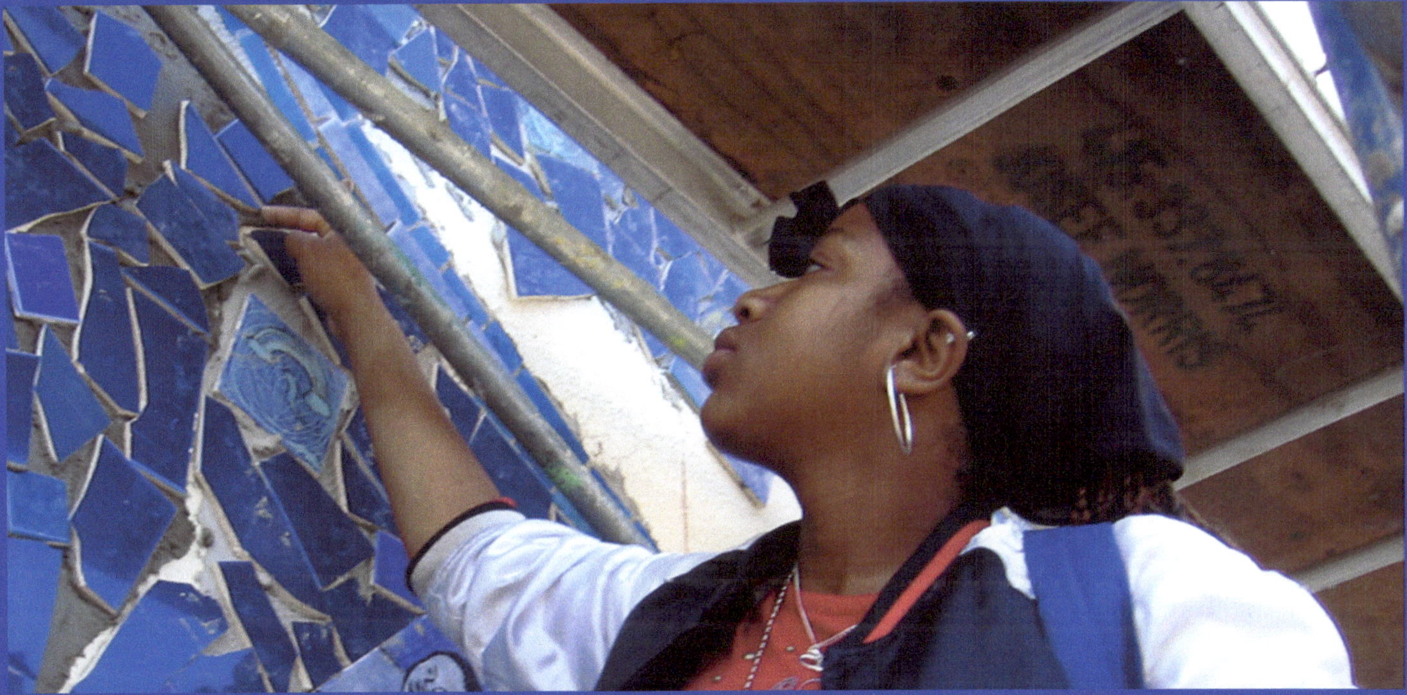

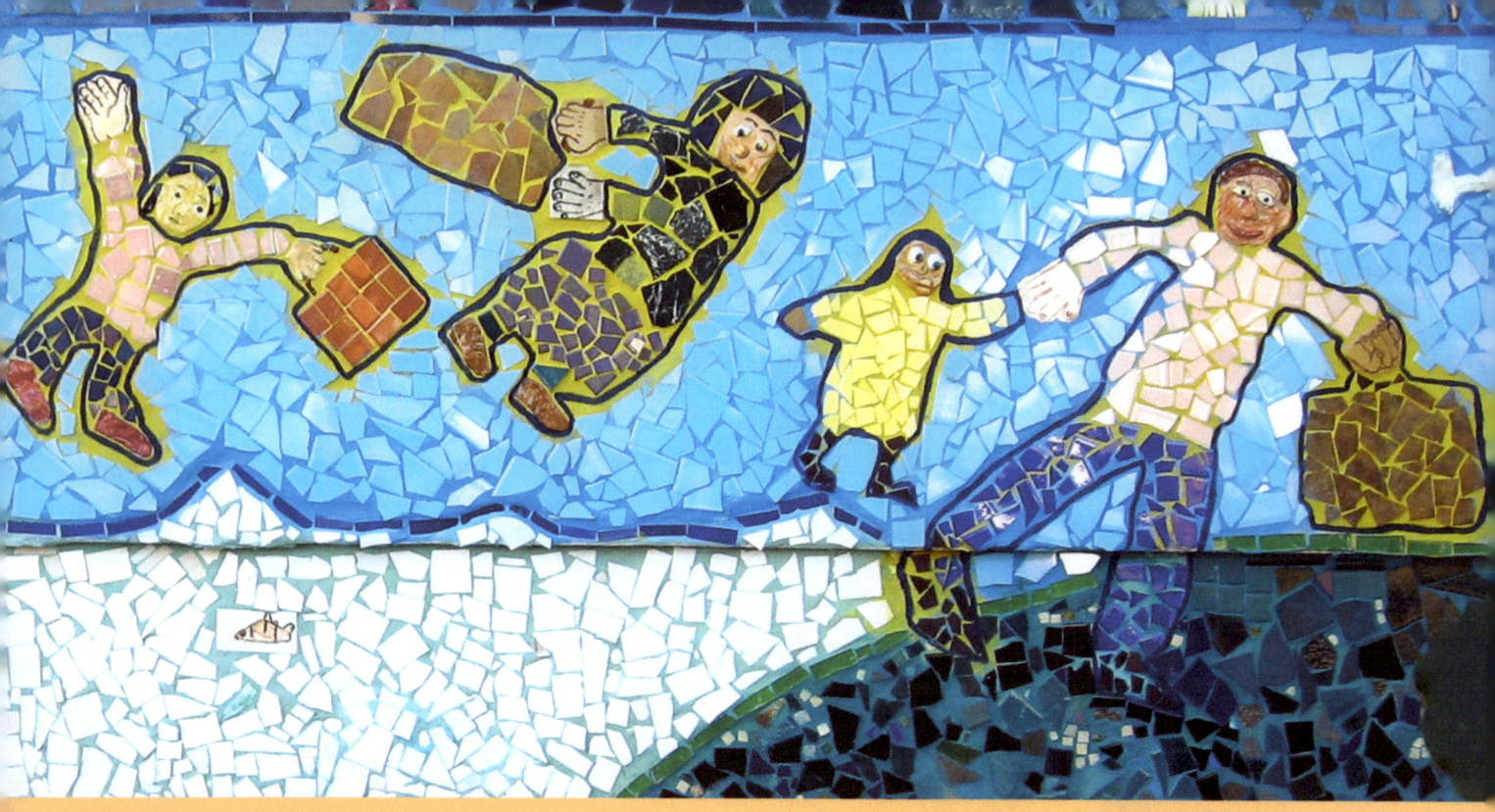

The Passport Project

The students of Mr. Aquerelli's 4th grade class at Jefferson Elementary School chose to do a mural about San Francisco. Because 4th grade social studies curriculum involves immigration, the teacher steered much of the research toward this subject, and how immigrants shape our city. We quickly discovered that every child in the class had either a parent or grandparent that came from another country. Each student had to develop a series of questions to ask a member of their family. They would then bring several items and make a classroom presentation.

Many of the students have parents who came from China, but they didn't know exactly where. Four of the students came from the former Soviet Union. Two of the students' families were from Kiev, and learned their family left for the U.S. because of the

Chernobyl accident. One student was from Iran, another from India, and another from Japan. Three of the students came from Laos and Vietnam. Their families came to San Francisco in the 1970's.

Students were asked to find out what kinds of jobs, hobbies and skills their families did in their home countries. One student, Lia wrote about her grandmother, who made umbrellas in the Ukraine. This image made it onto the mural.

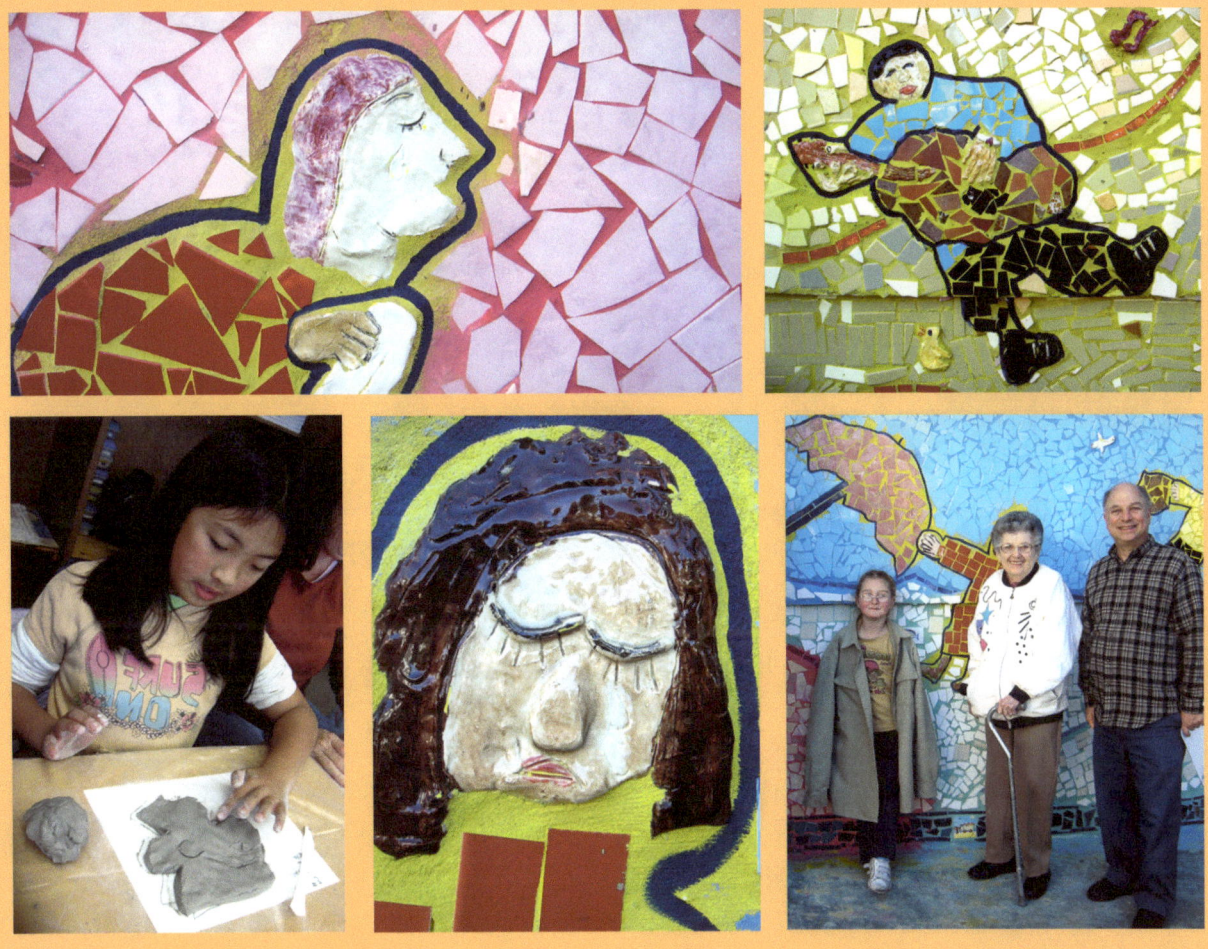

Each student created specific ceramic pieces for the mural.

Lia with her grandmother at the mural unveiling.

The Mural Making Process
Good Partnerships

The success of a Kid Serve project depends on strong partnerships - with a principal and the right teacher. I once cancelled a $10,000 project because the principal was not available to meet with me.

A great partnership is when you have a teacher and principal who are genuinely excited and share your vision of what this mural can mean for their kids and the entire school. I never approach a school with a theme. The mural theme is linked to the teacher's curriculum, which offers an amazing opportunity for them to bring their ideas and talents to the table.

For 4th grade immigration curriculum, Mr. Aquerelli, had his students interview their parents and grandparents about how they came to America. He wanted his students to discover their own stories in the immigration history they were studying.

Ms. Obregon wanted her 5th graders to become excited about a feminist labor hero who was still fighting for the rights of migrant workers.

These teachers were instrumental in pushing their kids to put their hearts into these murals - and in the process helped create some very interesting public art.

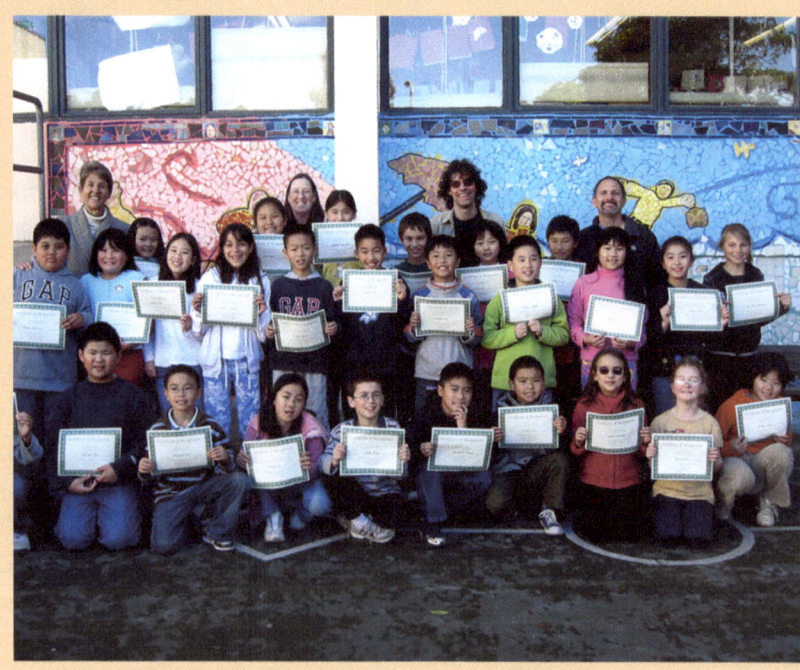

The mural unveiling for the "Passport Project"

42

Designing the Mural - creating the pieces of the mosaic puzzle

During a classroom assignment, we do an art project related to what the students are studying. For example, the students from one class went on a field trip to Muir Woods. After a 10-minute classroom discussion about the animals that live in this forest, the 3rd graders created tiles featuring their favorite animal. These tiles were then fired in a kiln and incorporated into the finished mural. Mosaic murals are like giant jigsaw puzzles. These exercises gave us actual pieces of this puzzle and created more opportunities for the students to have ownership in the finished mural.

After a few weeks of creating artwork, we have a "cut and paste" day, where students talk about the things they want to have on their mural. As the curriculum is integrated into the project, this is a great way to have the kids reflect on what they've been studying. Students take turns cutting out some of their drawings and placing them on butcher paper at the front of class. We conclude with a discussion of the images that should be removed and the ones that should remain.

We don't worry if a child is disappointed about not getting their drawing into the final design, because there will be many other ways for kids to have ownership in their mural.

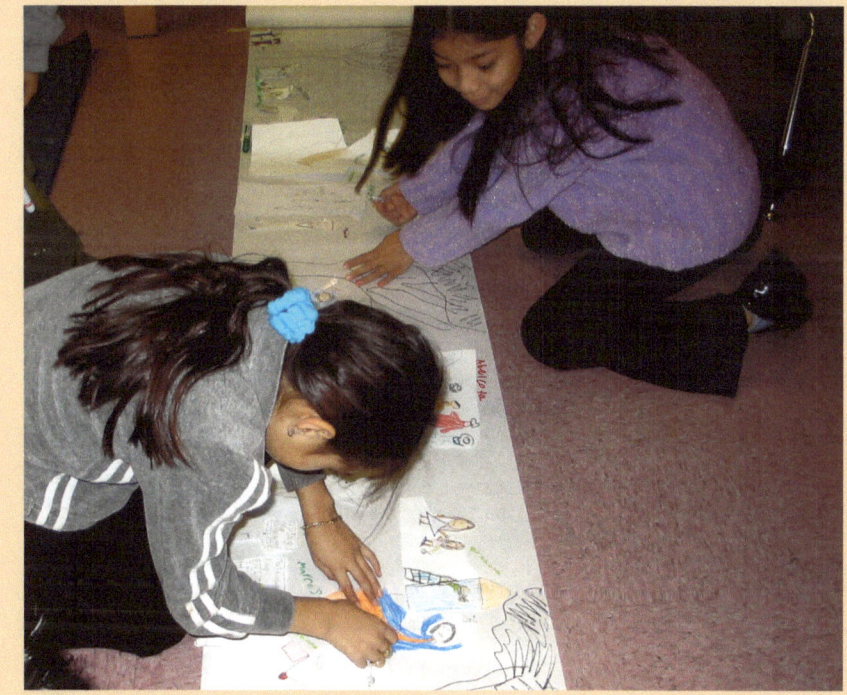

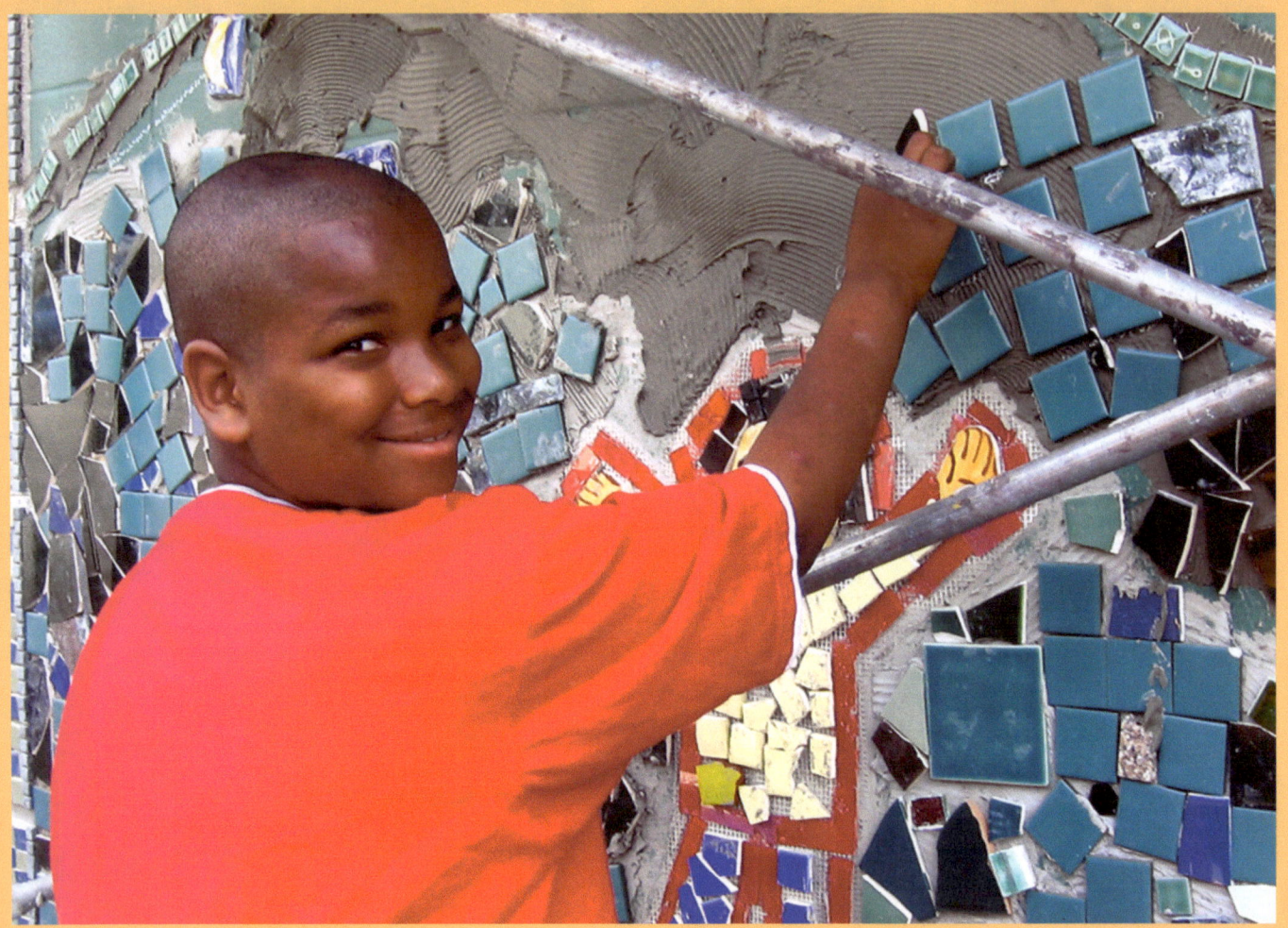

Ownership

Kid Serve projects are ultimately about ownership. If the child feels ownership in the artwork they're making, and the artwork is linked to their curriculum, the child can have a greater sense of ownership in their education. If the artwork is out in their neighborhood - they can have ownership in their communities. The pride and responsibility that goes with that ownership can change a child's relationship with their school, their teachers and their world.

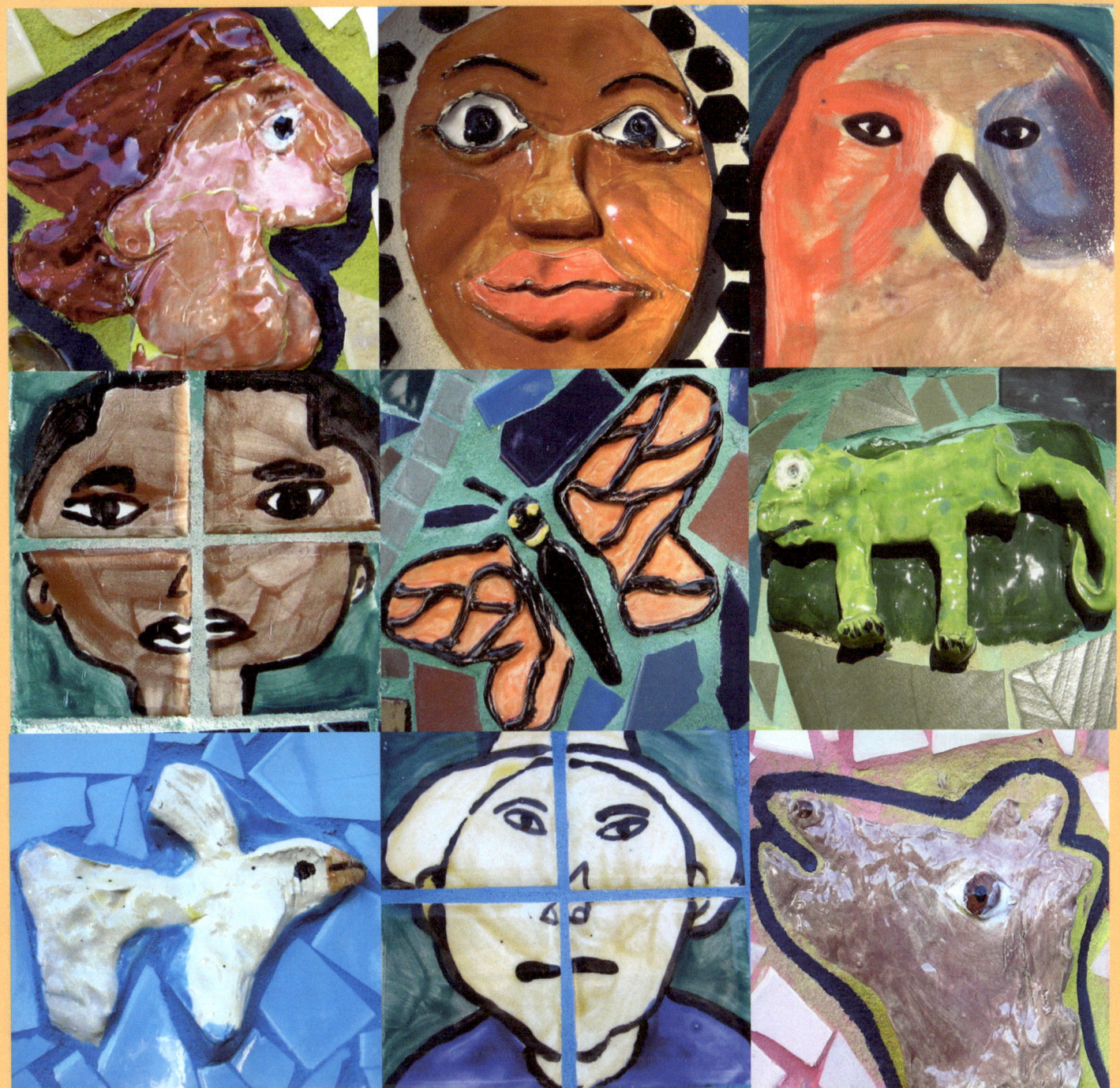

45

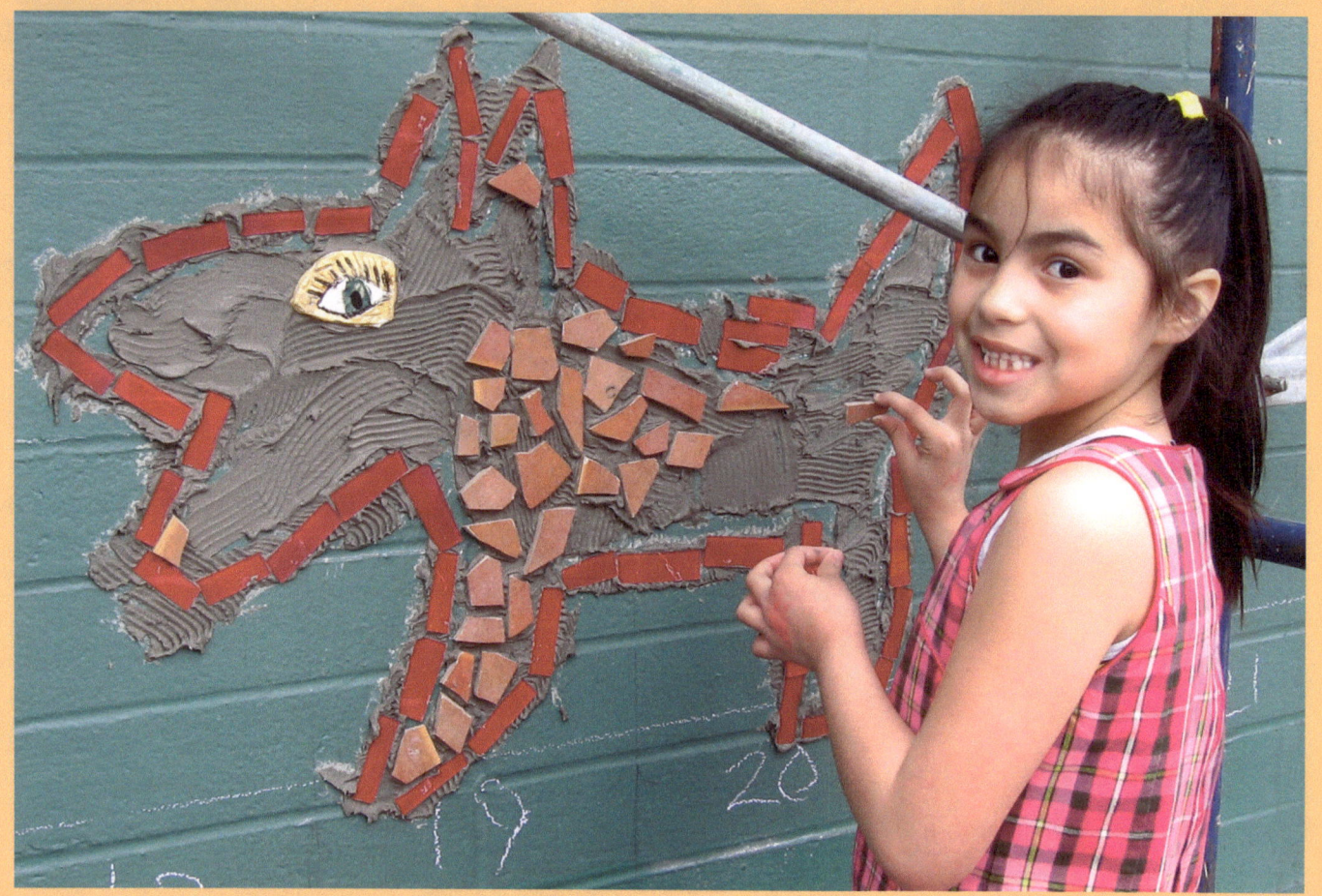

Laying the tile

After the principal and teachers approve the design, we are ready to start creating our mural. I usually work with small groups of 6 to 8 kids at a time in 35 minute shifts. This is a good amount of time for kids to stay focused. My goal is to have each child work on the mural at least 3 times during the residency.

I lay out sections of thinset mortor on the wall and have the kids place specific tiles into that area. I tell kids to lay the tile like they're building a brick wall - working out from one area, so the pieces are close together.

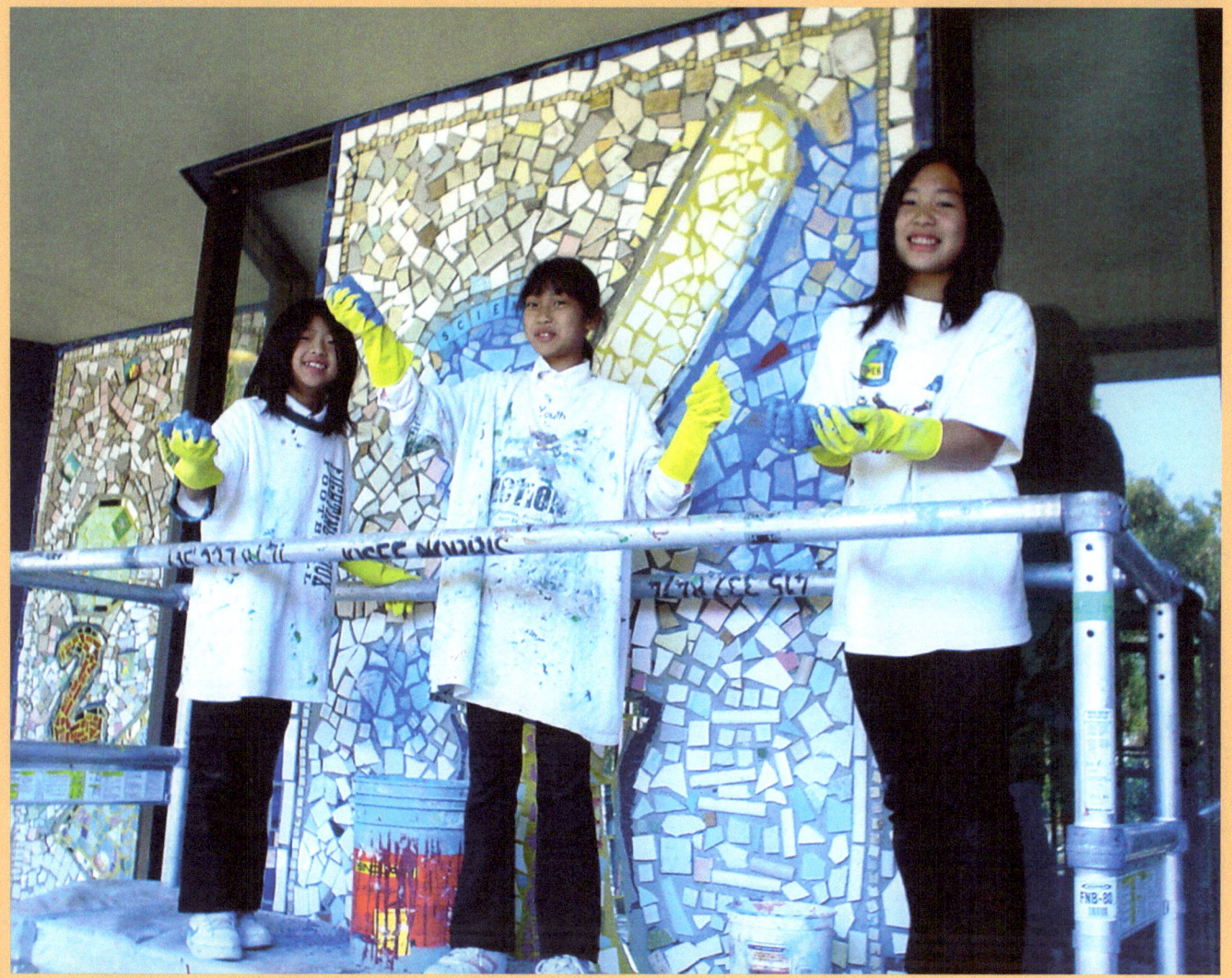

Grouting

Equipped with cloth and latex gloves to protect their hands, students mix painter's tint into sand and cement and apply grout on to their mural. The color of the grout can help bring out figures in the foreground. This is a very popular activity with the kids.

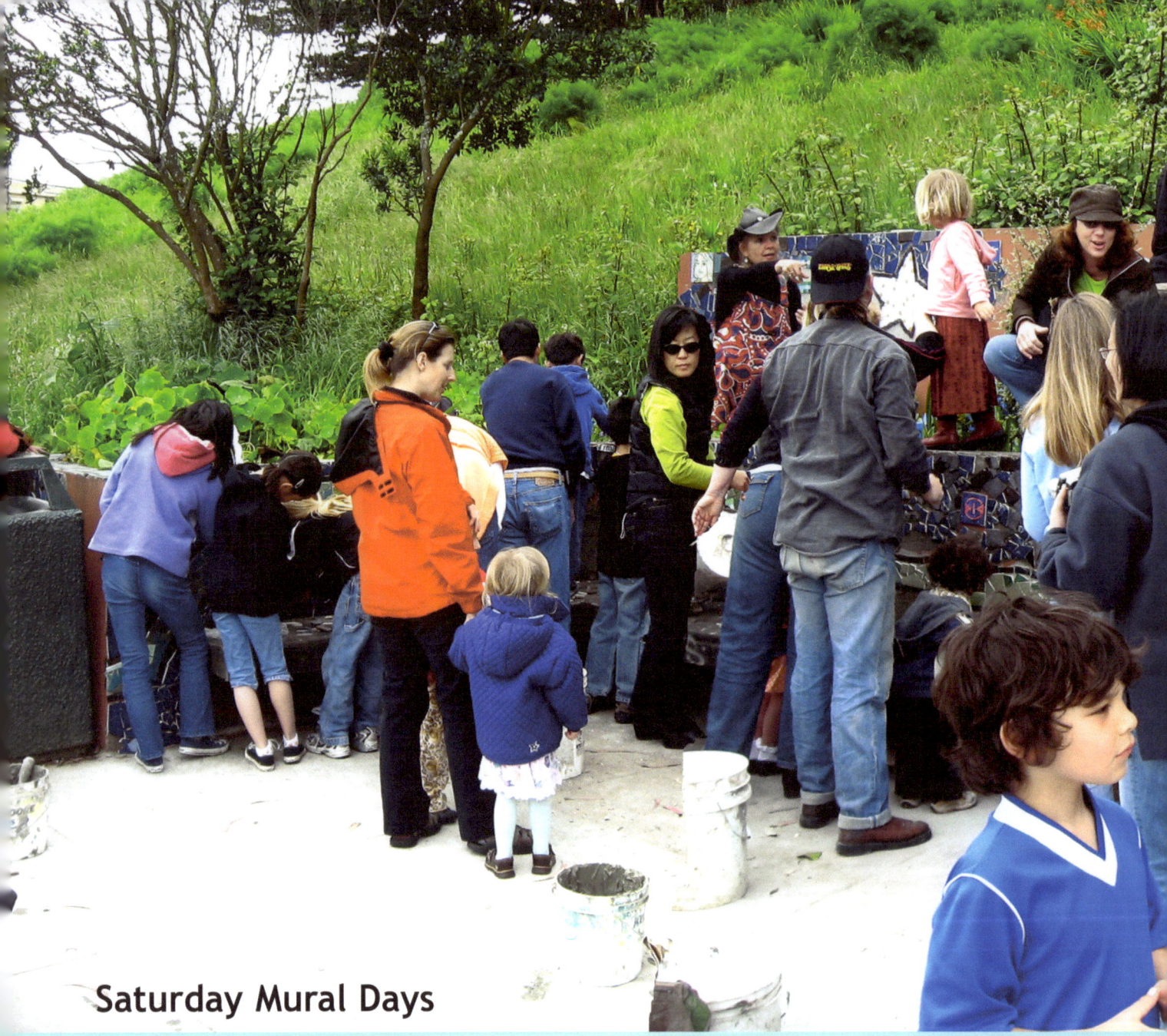

Saturday Mural Days

Several times a year we do Saturday Mural Days, to give parents, friends and kids from

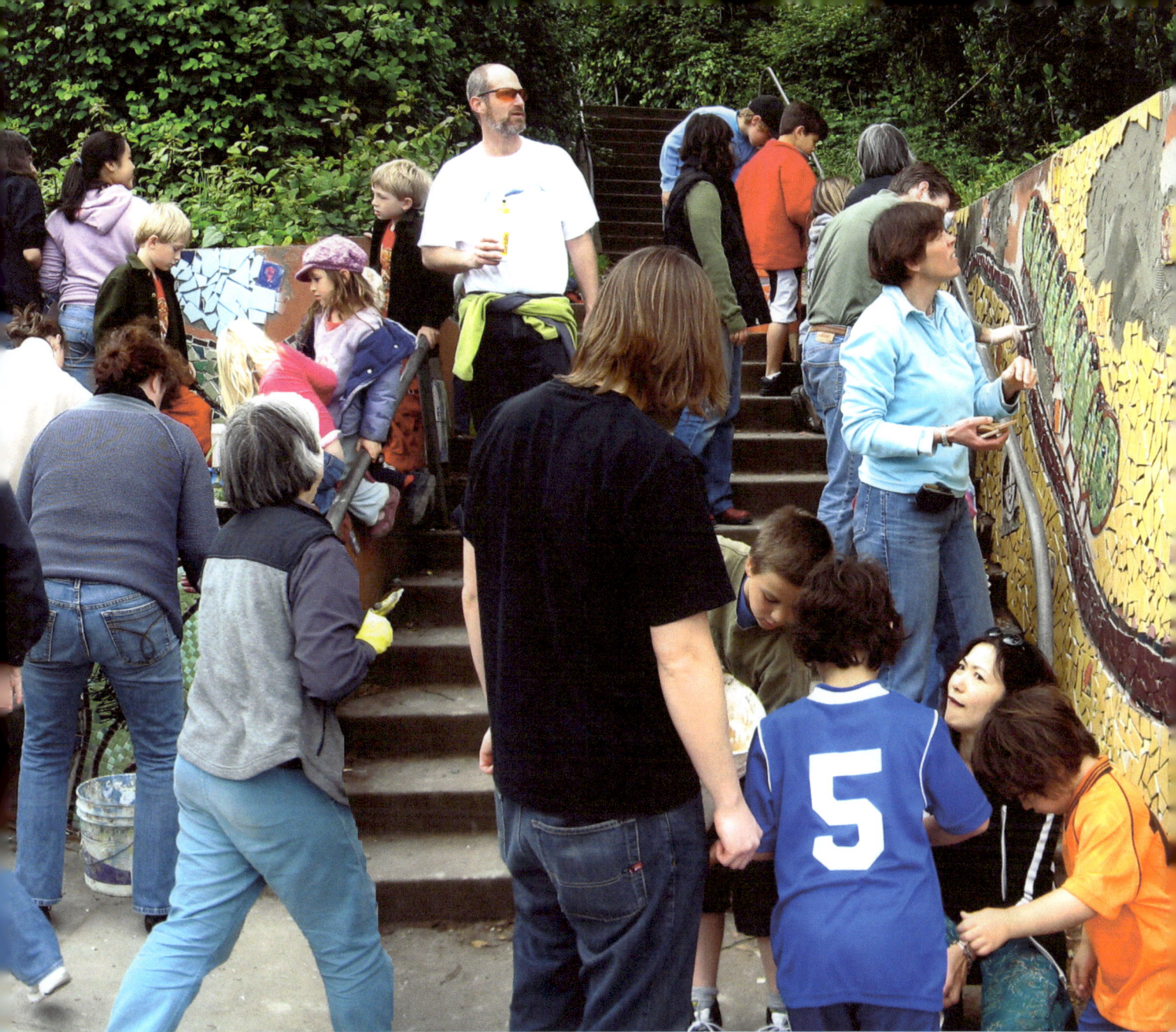

other classes a chance to work on the mural. This makes the mural making process more of a community event.

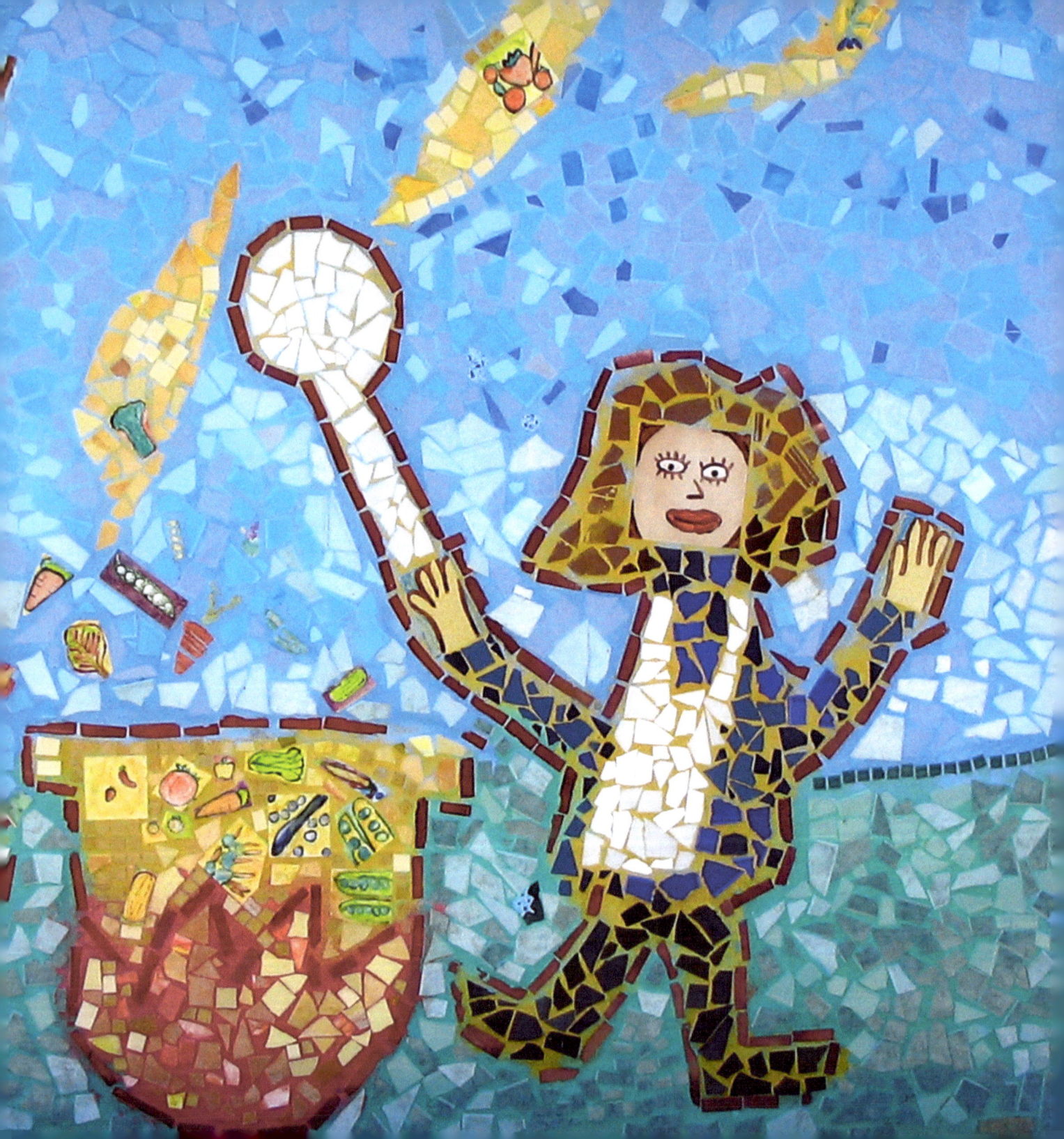

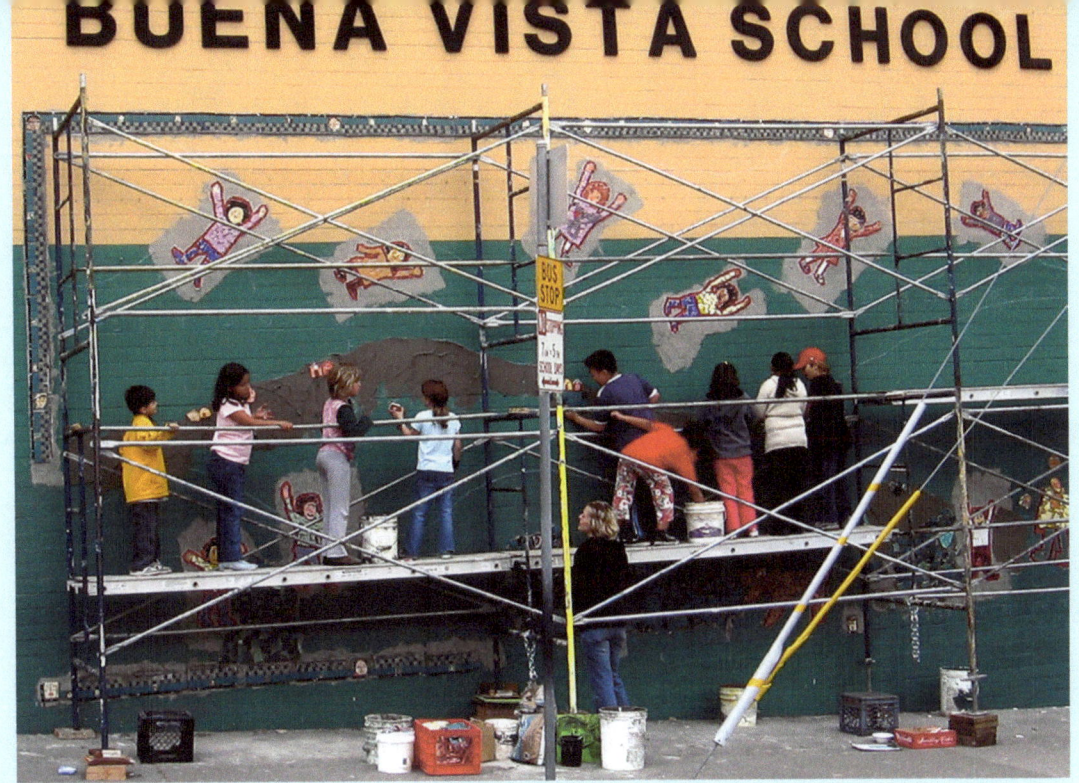

What is Service-Learning?

Kid Serve uses the 8 elements of Service-Learning to direct our projects. These include:

Community involvement - Through Saturday Mural Days and Unveilings, community volunteers and guest speakers

Solving a specific need - The children evaluate how a public art project may improve their neighborhood

Civic responsibility - How is this project being of service?

Integrating curriculum - The project facilitates the teaching of the curriculum

Reflection - Art projects serve to reinforce the curriculum being taught

Evaluation - Students and instructors are involved in actively evaluating

Youth Voice - Wherever possible children direct every aspect of the project

Public Art - The completed project must be outside and visible to the community

51

"The Children's Botanical Garden"

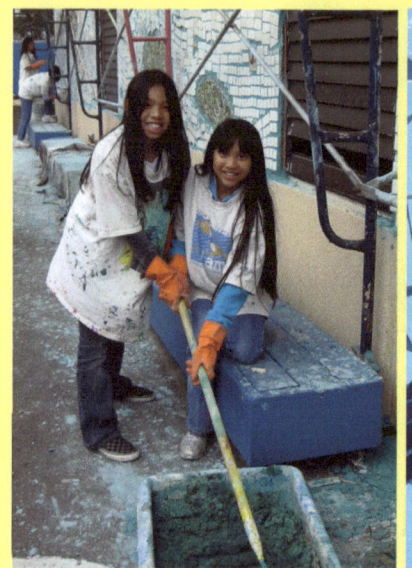
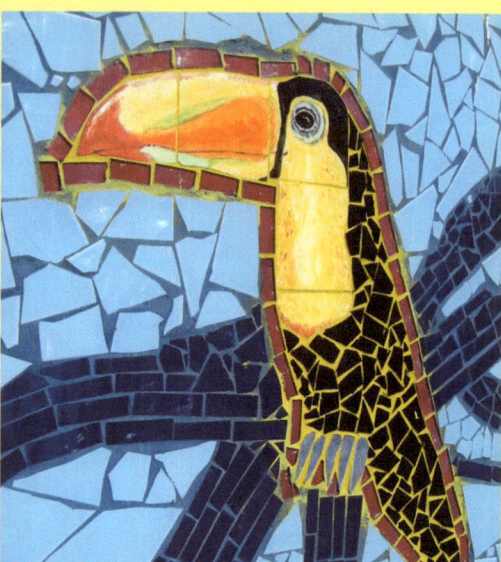
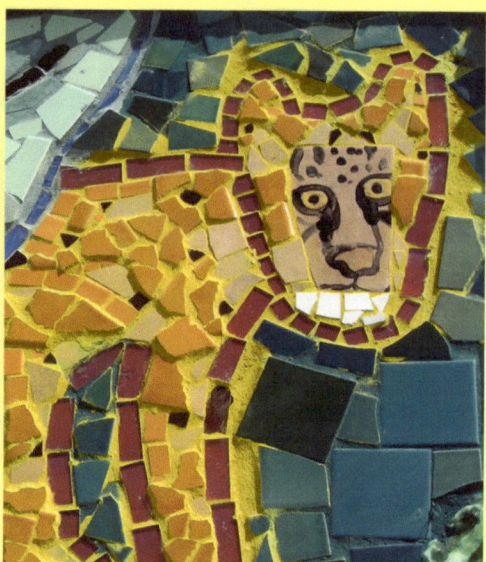
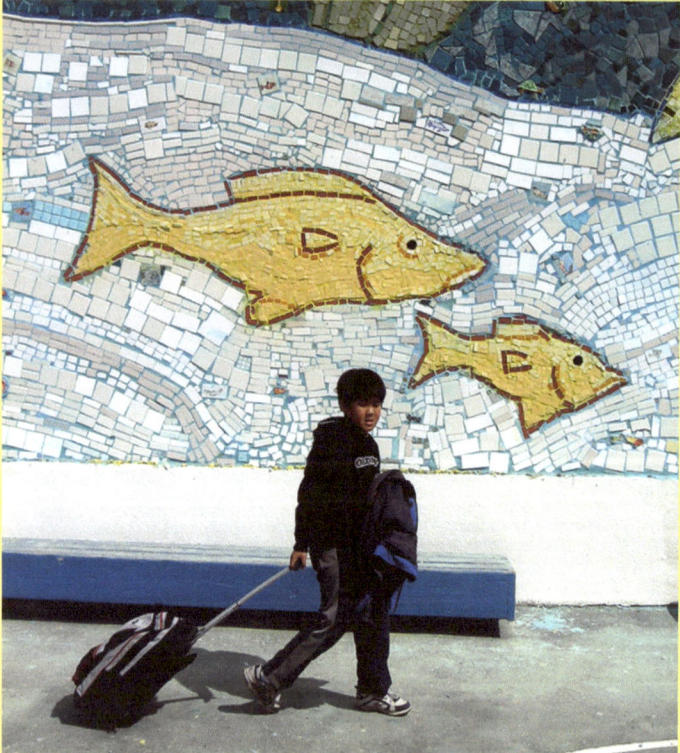
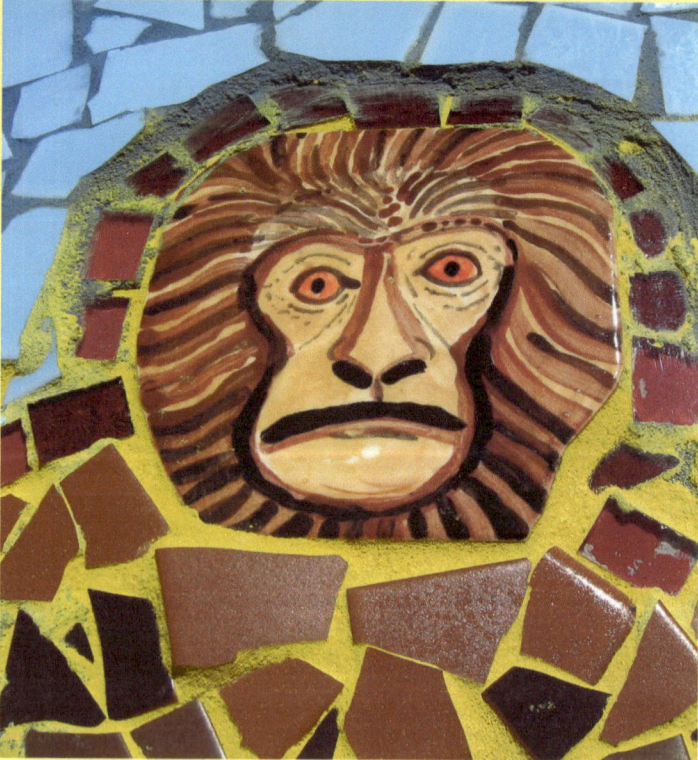

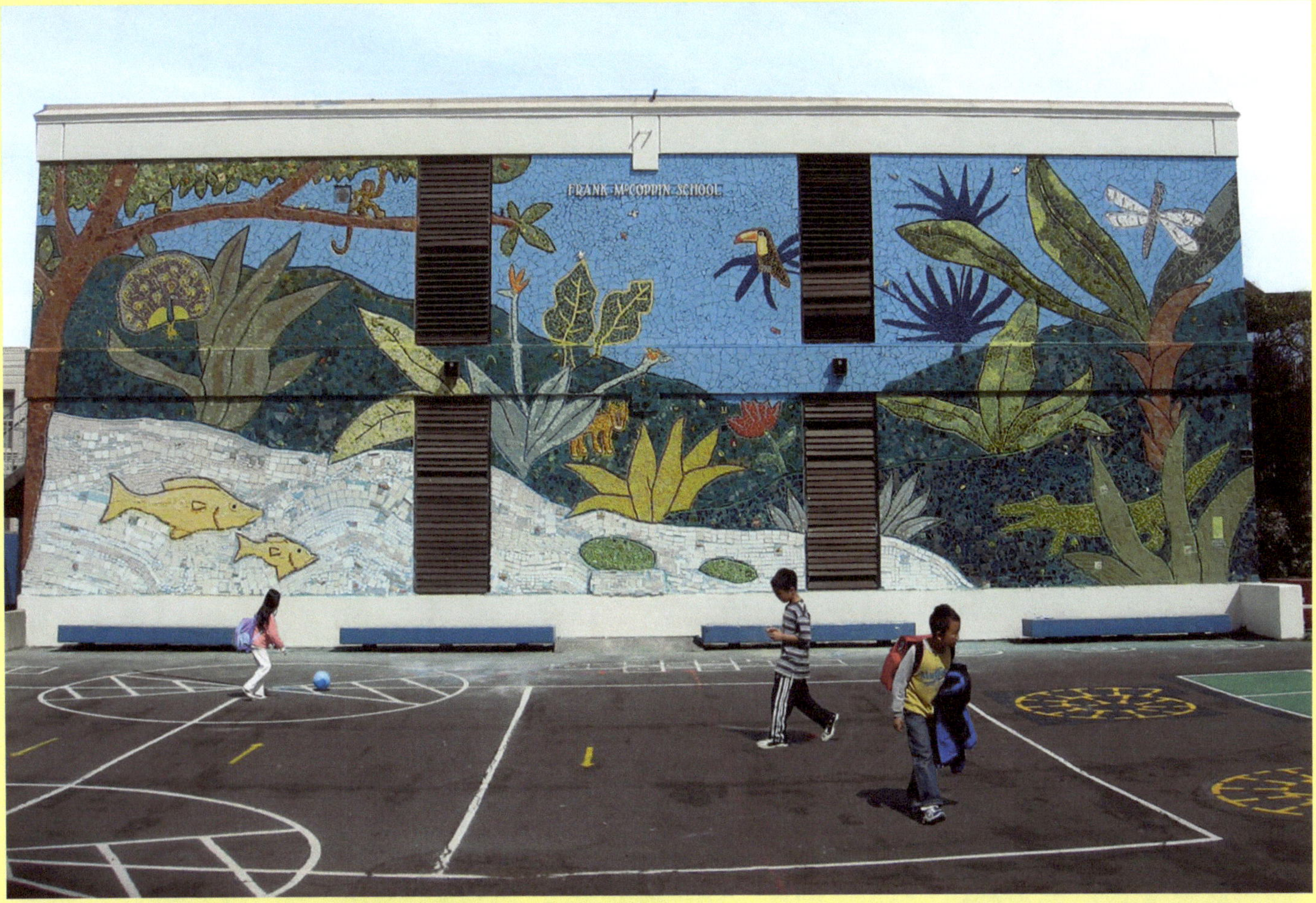

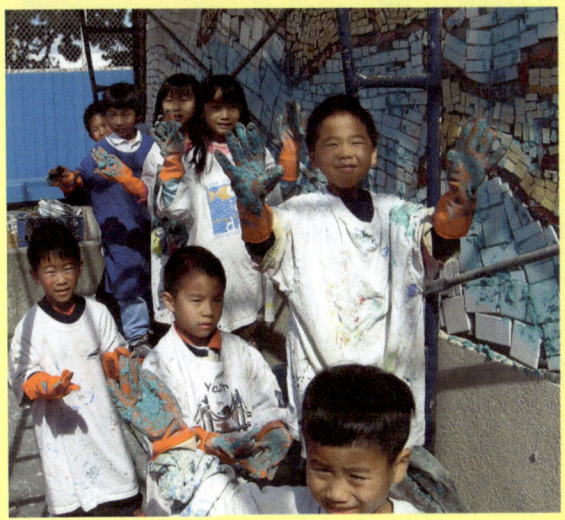
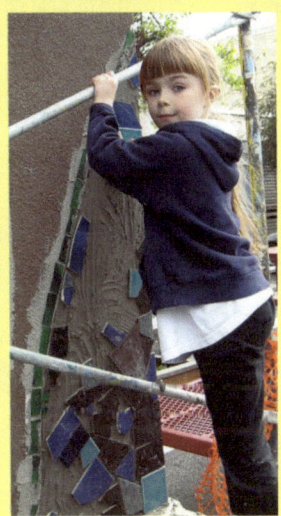
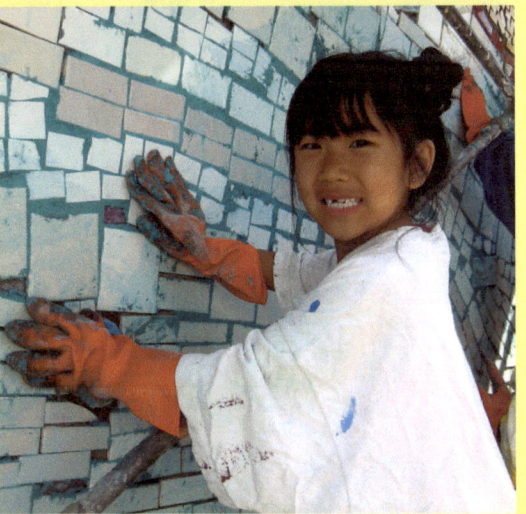

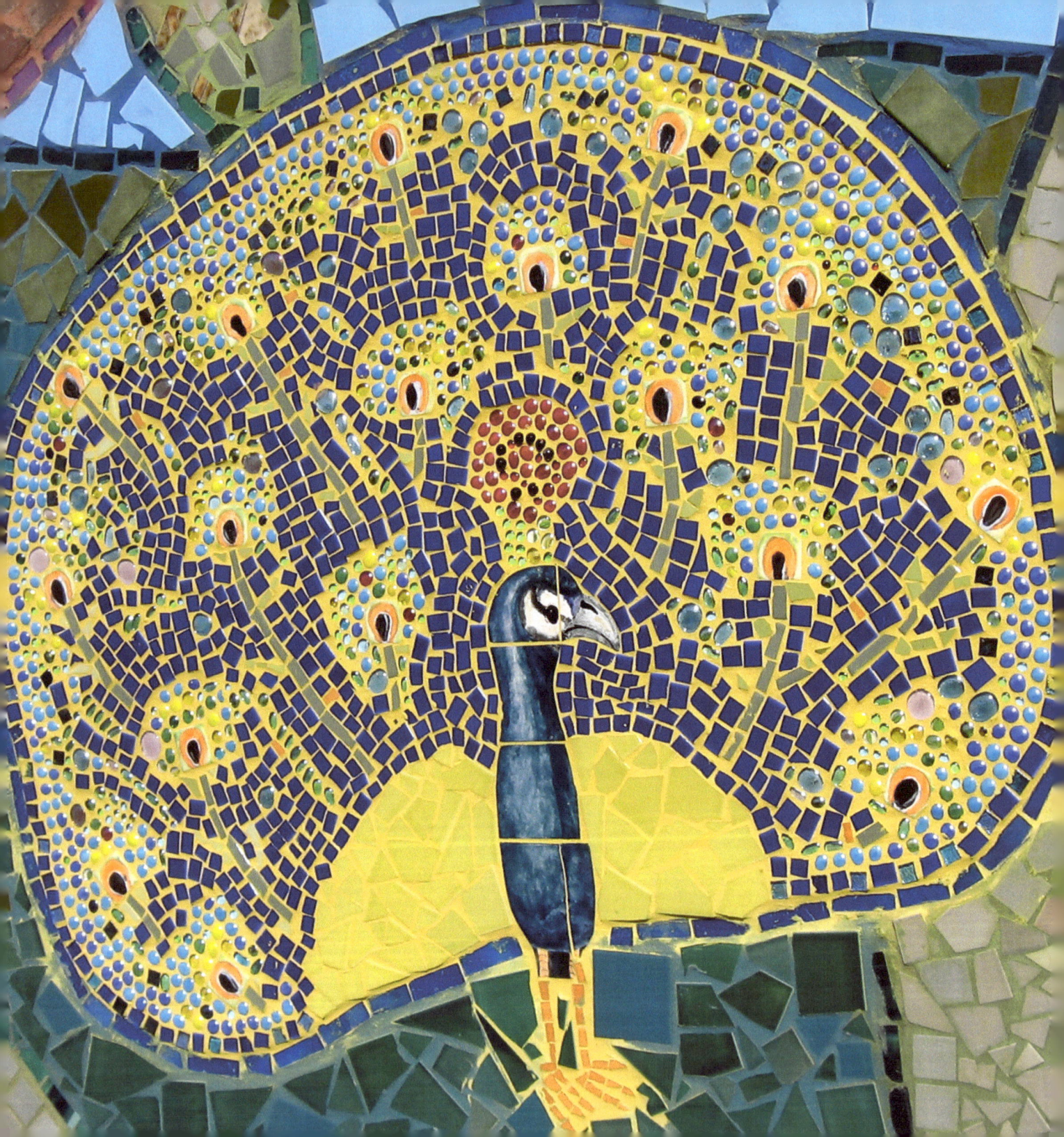

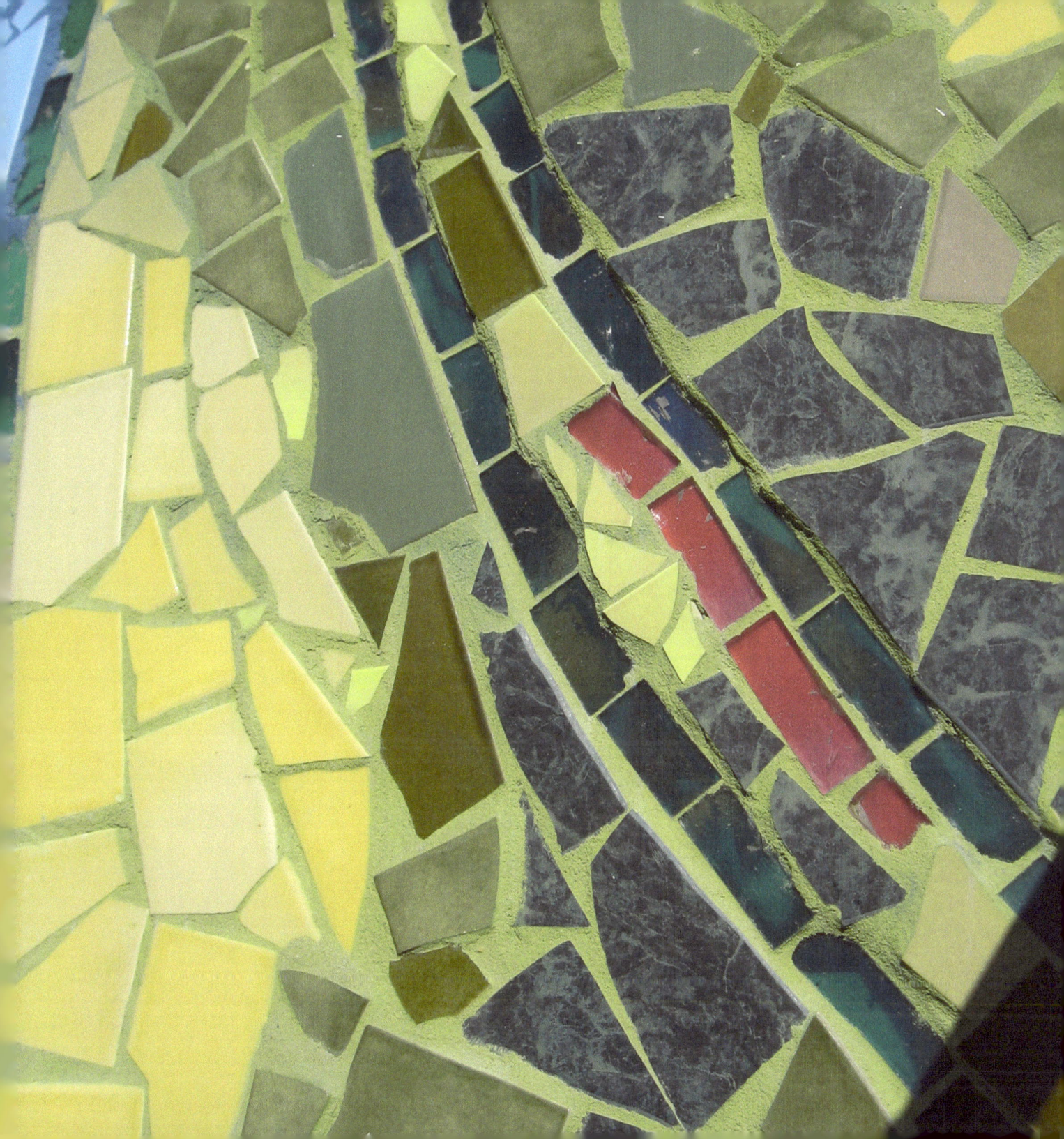

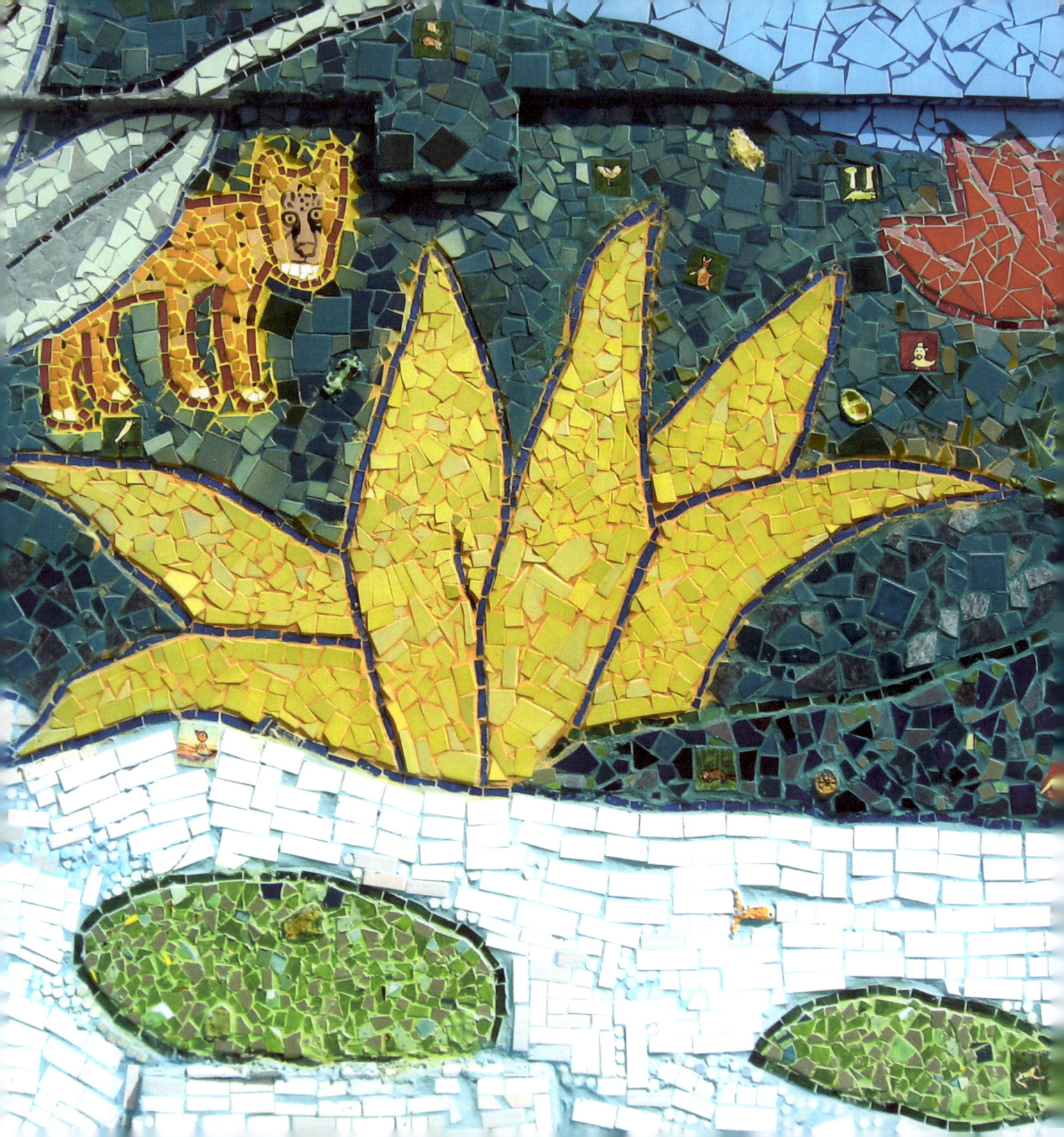

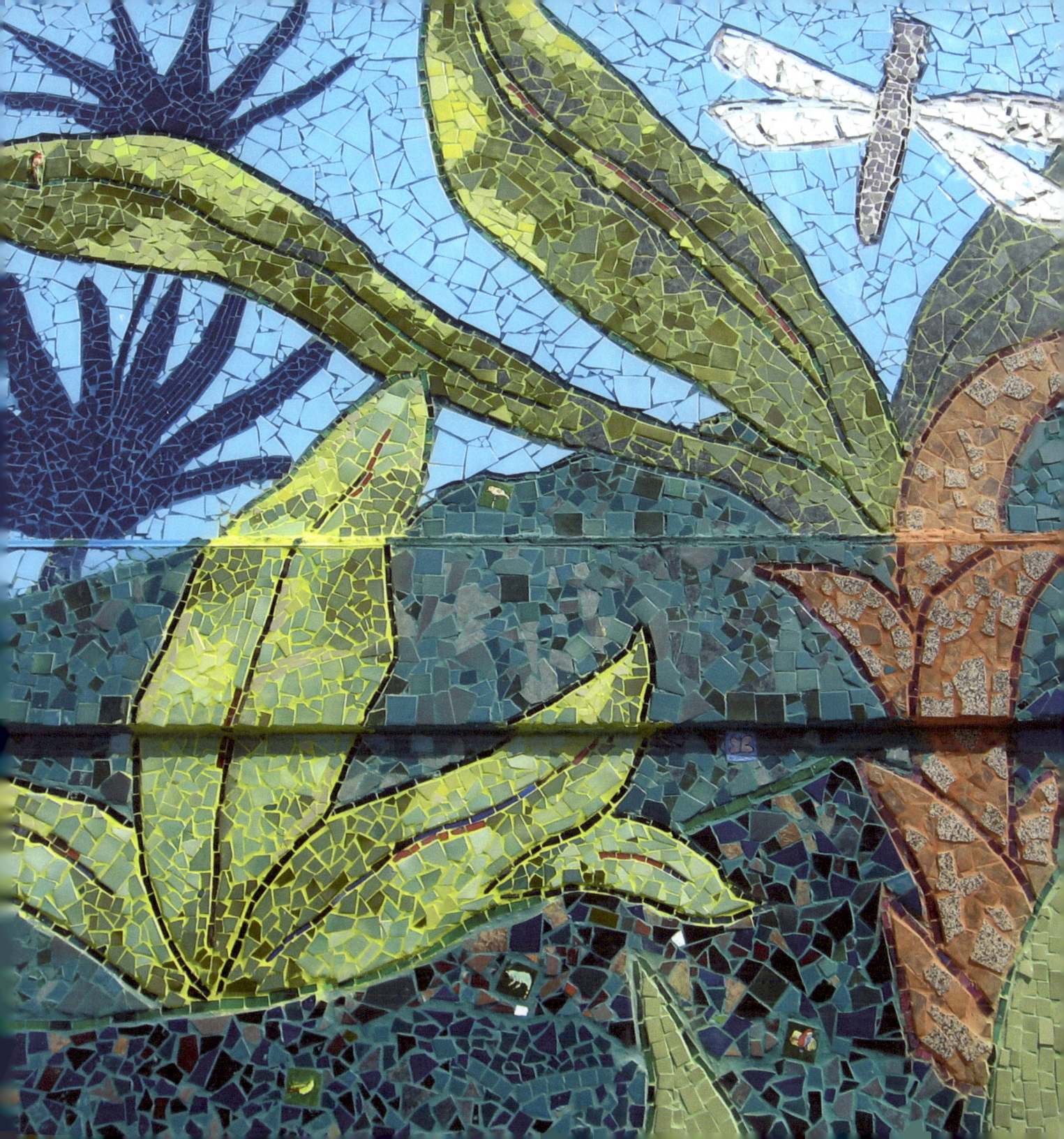

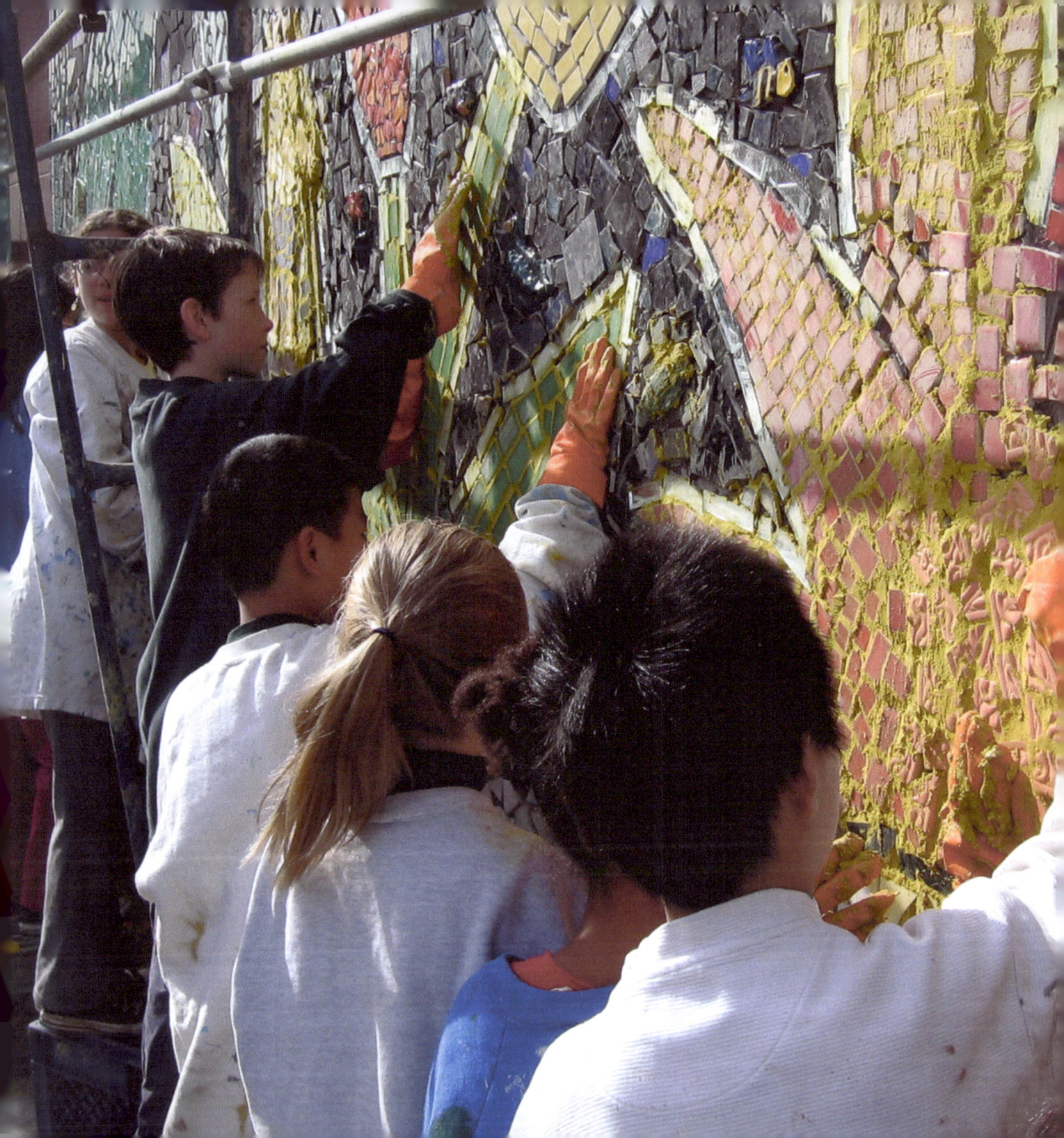

"Greening San Francisco"

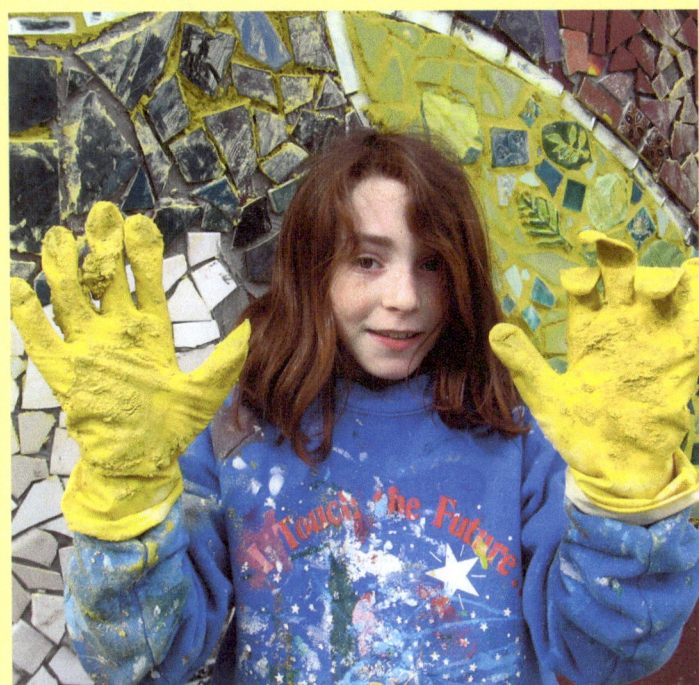

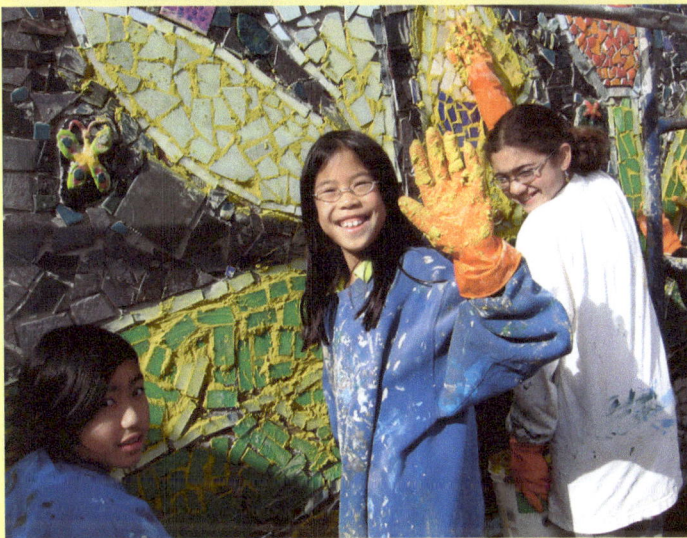

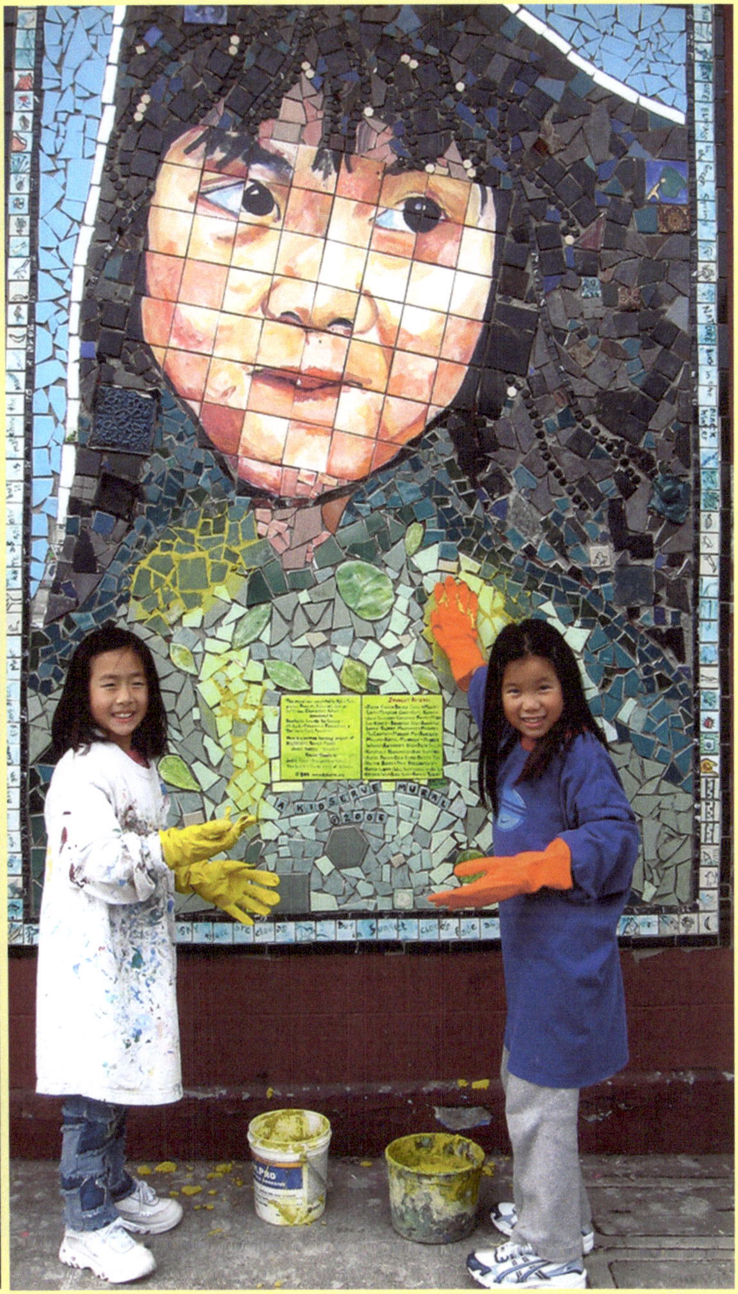

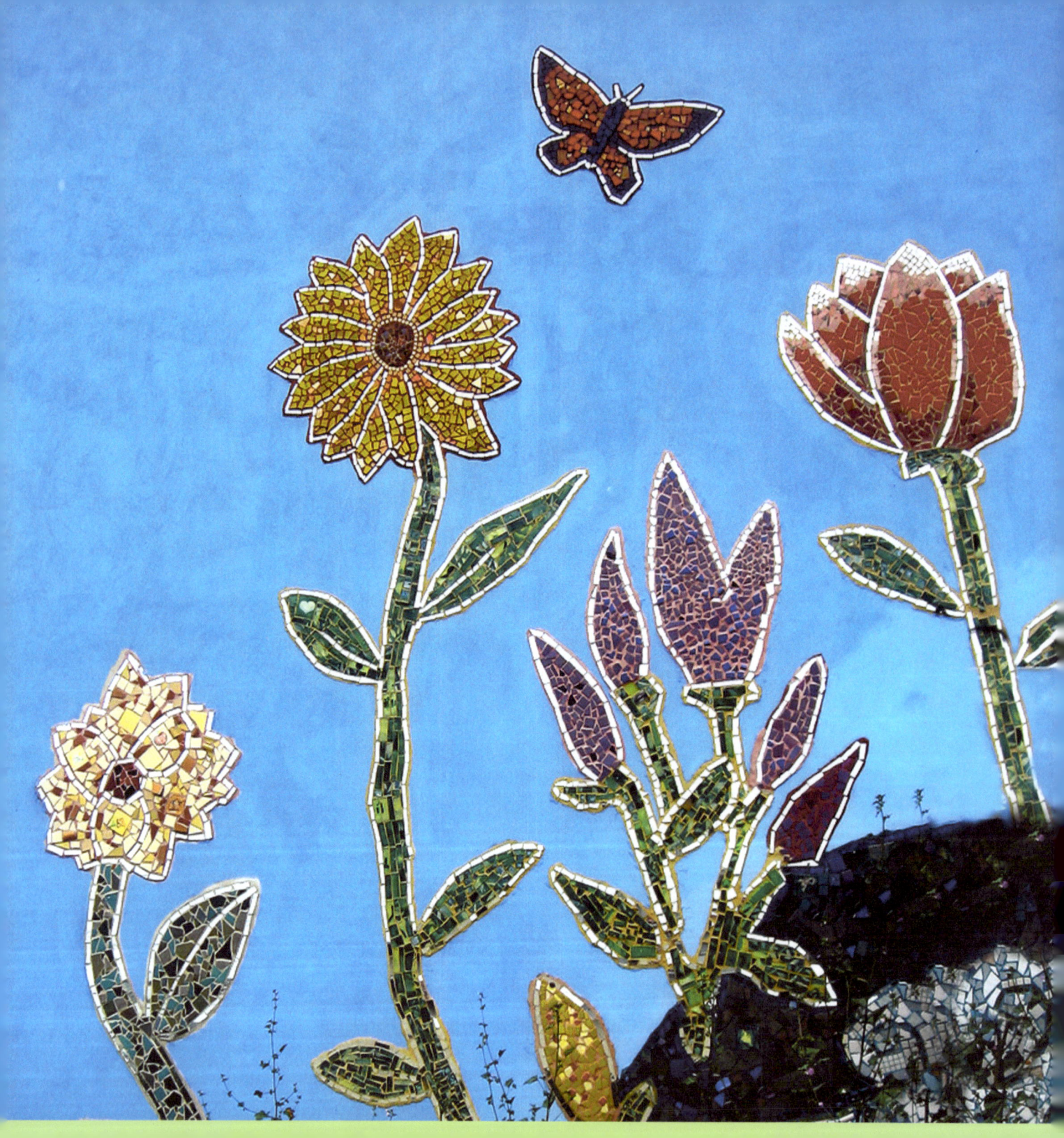

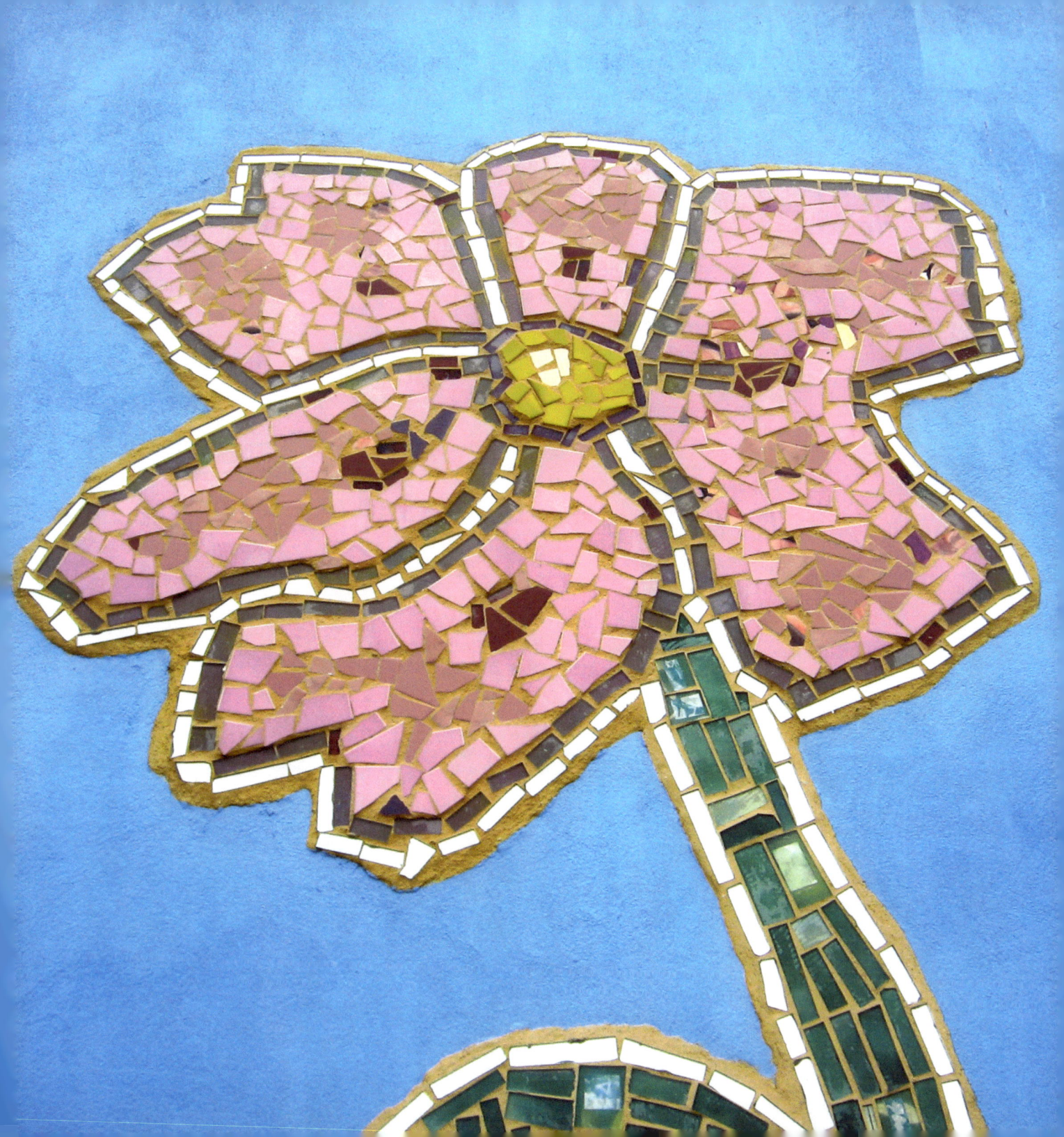

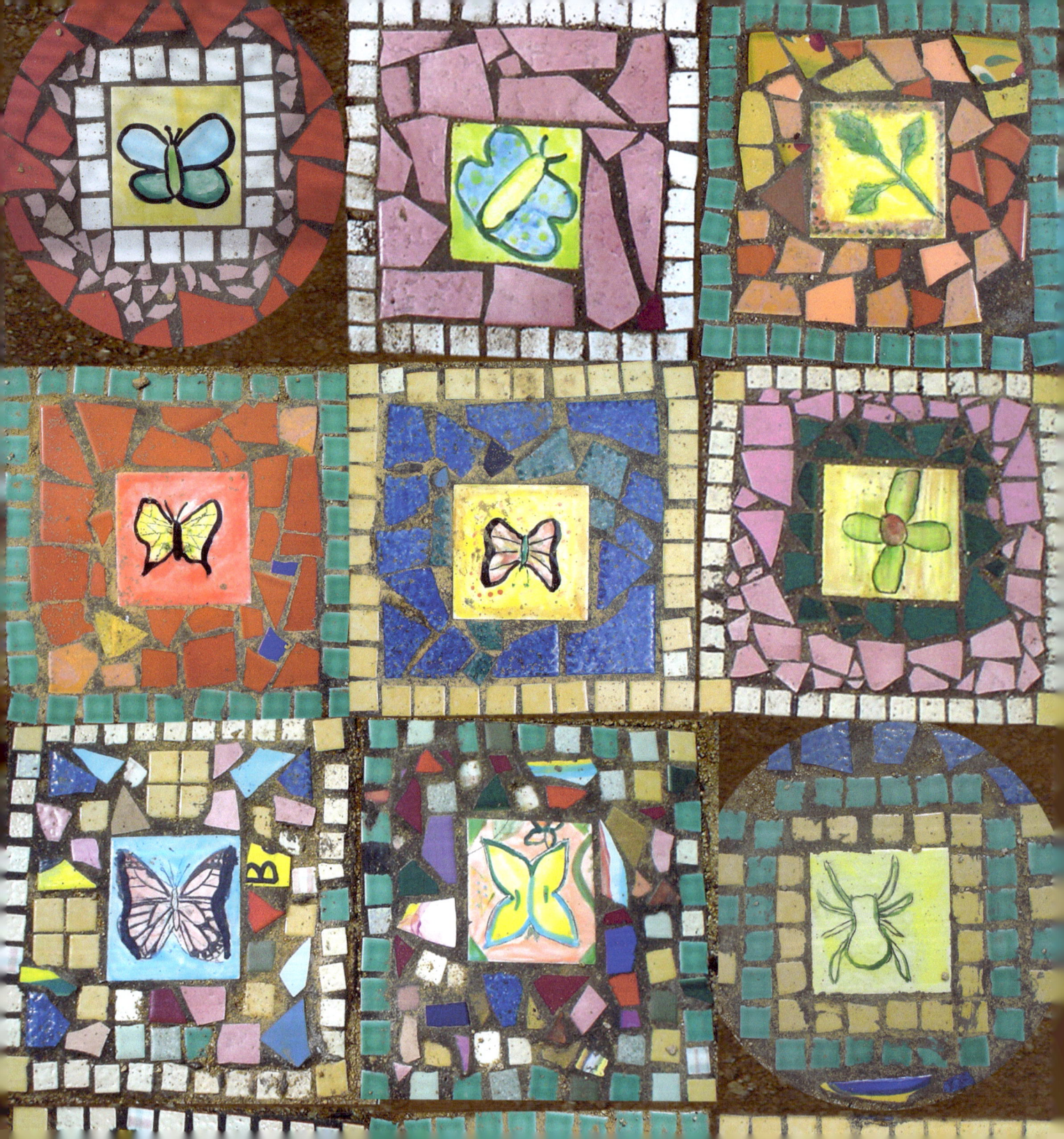

The Living Library
Stepping Stones

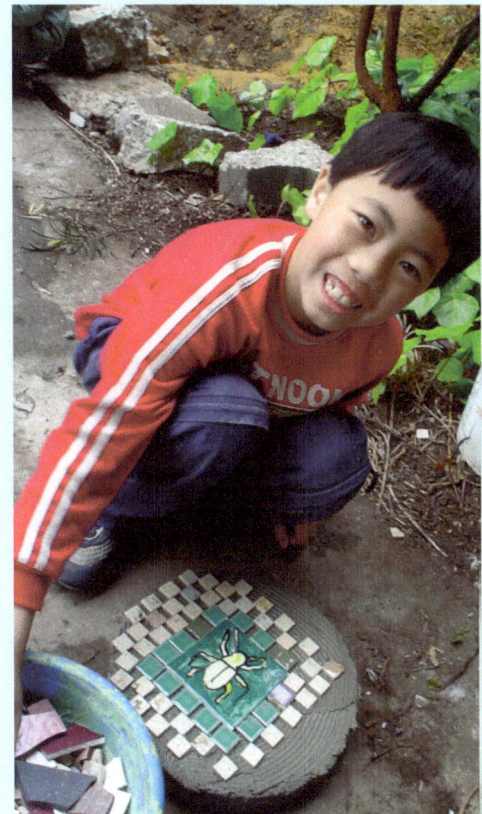

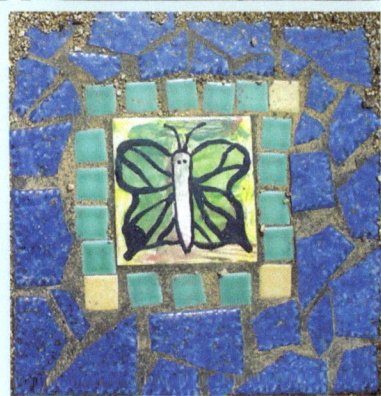

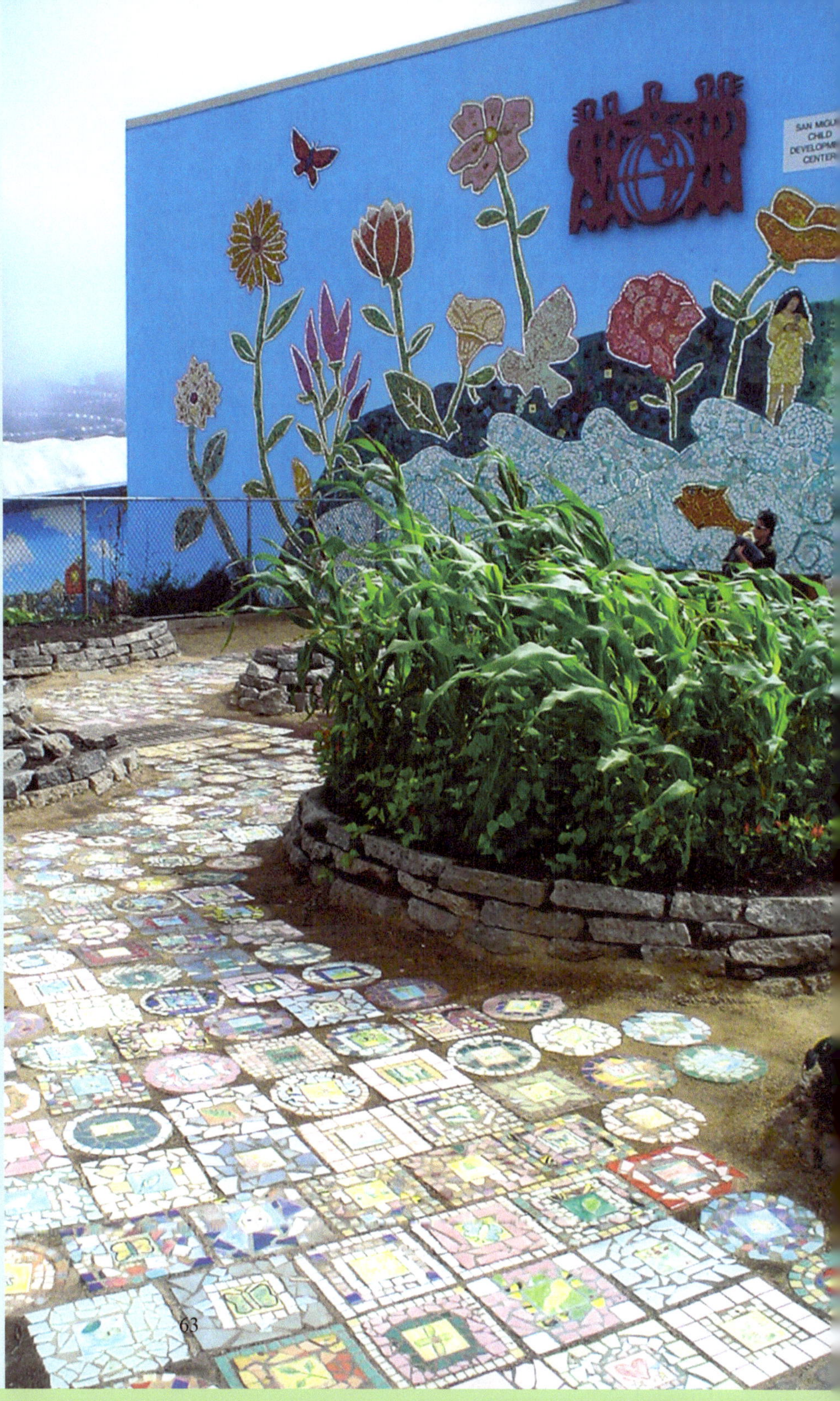

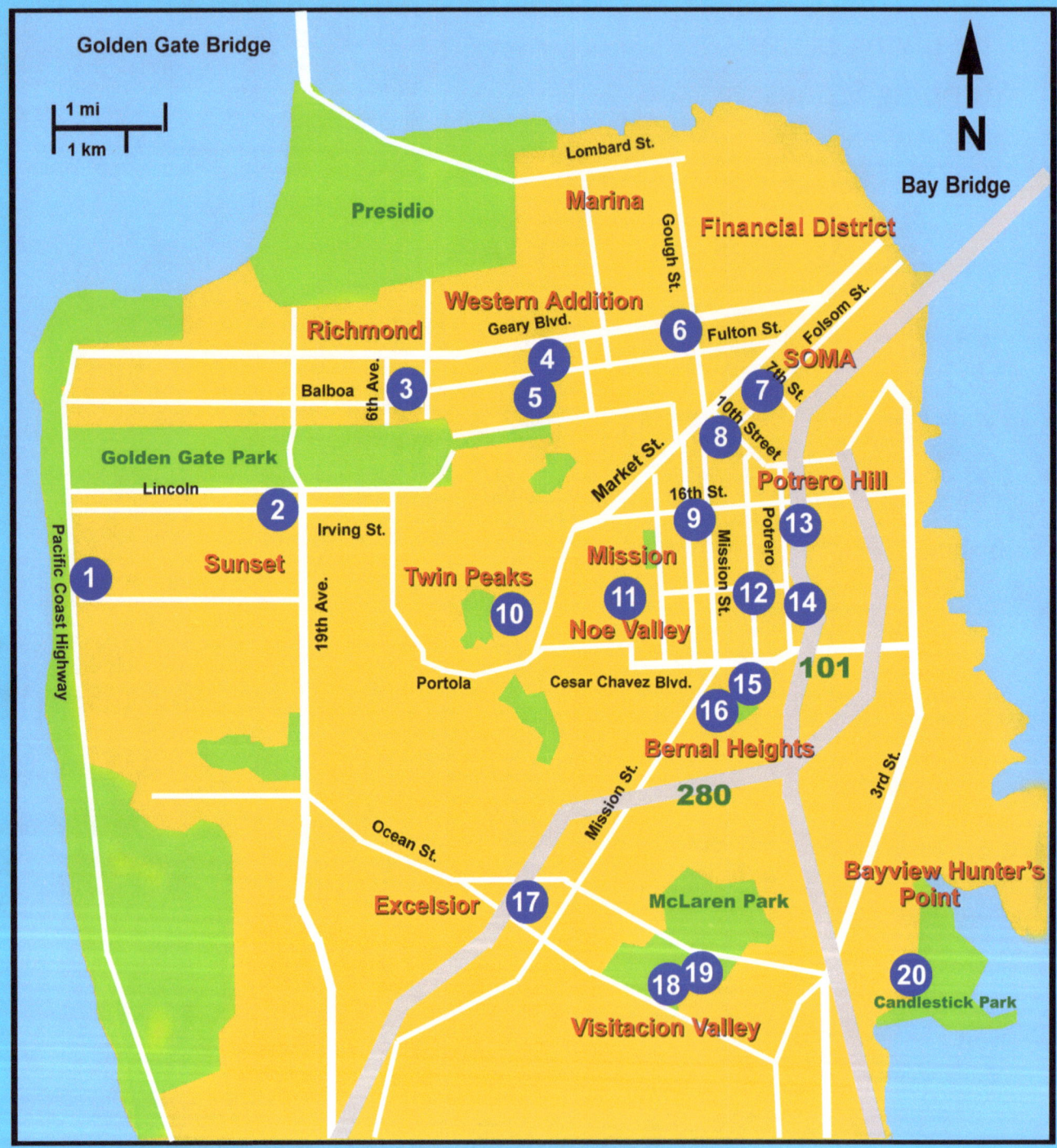

Golden Gate Bridge

1 mi
1 km

Presidio

Marina

Financial District

Bay Bridge

N

Western Addition

Richmond

Geary Blvd.

Fulton St.

6

SOMA

Folsom St.

Balboa

6th Ave.

3

4

5

7

7th St.

10th Street

Gough St.

Lombard St.

8

Golden Gate Park

Lincoln

Market St.

16th St.

Potrero Hill

13

2

Irving St.

9

Mission

12

14

Sunset

19th Ave.

Twin Peaks

11

Mission St.

Potrero

Noe Valley

10

15

101

Portola

Cesar Chavez Blvd.

16

Pacific Coast Highway

Bernal Heights

280

Ocean St.

Mission St.

3rd St.

Bayview Hunter's Point

Excelsior

17

McLaren Park

18 19

20

Candlestick Park

Visitacion Valley

1. **"The Julia Butterfly Mural"** Sunset Elementary School 41st Ave & Ortega Street

2. **"Greening San Francisco" & "The Passport Project"** Starbucks Store at 19th & Irving Streets

3. **"Children's Botanical Garden"** Frank McCoppin Elementary School 651 6th Ave. (between Cabrillo & Balboa Sts.)

4. **"Hope" & "The Urban Portrait Project"** Geary Blvd. (between Scott & Steiner Streets)

5. **"Mosaic Animal Sculptures"** 1601 Turk St. (at Pierce Street)

6. **"The Performing Arts Garage"** Gough & Fulton Streets near Civic Center

7. **"Bessie Carmichael Mural"** 375 7th Street (School between Folsom & Harrison Streets)

8. **"Children's Village"** 250 10th St. (between Folsom & Howard Streets)

9. **"Our Children"** 66 Hoff Street (between 16th & 17th Sts, one block west of Mission Streets)

10. **"Rooftop Murals"** 433 Burnett & 500 Corbett Streets (2 murals - 2 campuses)

11. **"Sea Turtle"** James Lick Middle School 25th Street at Castro Street.

12. **"Buena Vista"** Buena Vista School 2641 25th Street (between Utah and Potrero Streets)

13. **"California Oral Histories"** 655 De Haro Street (between 18th & 19th Streets)

14. **"Civil Rights Heroes" & "Our Ancestors"** Starr King Elementary School (23rd & Wisconsin Streets.)

15. **"A Tribute to Dolores Huerta" & "Native Stories"** Leonard R. Flynn Elementary School 3125 Cesar Chavez Blvd. (at Harrison Streets.)

16. **"Bernal Farm"** Junipero Serra Child Development Center 155 Appleton Street (between Mission St. & Holly Park Circle)

17. **"Suncatchers" & "A Living Library"** James Denman Middle School & San Miguel Children's Center. at 299 Oneida Ave (between Delano & San Jose Avenue)

18. **"The Diversity Mural"** Visitacion Valley Elementary School 55 Schwerin Street (at Visitacion)

19. **"Viz Valley Pride"** Visitacion Valley Middle School 450 Raymond Avenue.

20. **"Community Peace"** Bret Harte Elementary School 1035 Gilman Avenue.

Acknowledgements

Since our first mural workshop in 1999, I have partnered with over 80 teachers and school principals through out the Bay Area. Many of the teachers were the heart and soul of these projects. The finished murals are as much a landmark to their work in the classroom as they are to the work done by the kids. I would like to thank all of the parent volunteers and PTA's, who have become such a vitally important force in our inner city schools.

I would like to thank a number of arts administrators who were powerful allies for this program during its first year - specifically former Director Richard Newirth, Jewelle Gomez and the entire staff at the San Francisco Arts Commission. Many thanks to Wayne Cook at the California Arts Council, and Garrick Ramirez at the Every Child Can Learn Foundation (currently known as San Francisco School Alliance). I want to acknowledge the hard work of all the mural assistants over the years - especially Becca Norris, Sandee Manuel, and Erin Sorenson. Brad Hipkins and dozens of his colleagues at Starbucks Coffee Company have helped hundreds of students create their murals on buildings throughout the city.

I would like to thank the Kid Serve Board of Directors: Bev Ripps, Nan Torrey, Patty McManus, Irene Kelly, Rosie Scott, Christina Quiroz, Brad Hipkins and former development director Dyana Curreri-Ermatinger who have helped guide our small nonprofit since its inception.

Thanks to my family of educators, from university professors to school teachers and principals. And lastly, I want to thank my wife Jo, a choreographer and educator, and my 3 year old son Adi, who keeps teaching me new techniques in art making.

These mural projects have been made possible by generous support from:

Potrero Nuevo Fund (Tides Foundation)
Walter & Elise Haas Fund
San Francisco Foundation
Starbucks Coffee Company
Starbucks Foundation
City of San Francisco Community Challenge Grant
San Francisco Arts Commission
Trio Foundation
Gould Family Fund
Fitzpatrick Foundation
Yerba Buena Center for the Arts
Heath Ceramics

WestEd
Ideal Tile
Stanley Langendorf Foundation
Bernard & Alba Witkin Charitable Trust
Hasbro Children's Foundation
Nicholson Family Foundation
Stocker Foundation
Miranda Lux Foundation
California Council for the Humanities
VanLoenSels/Remberock Foundation
The Junior League
Stuart Foundation
California Arts Council

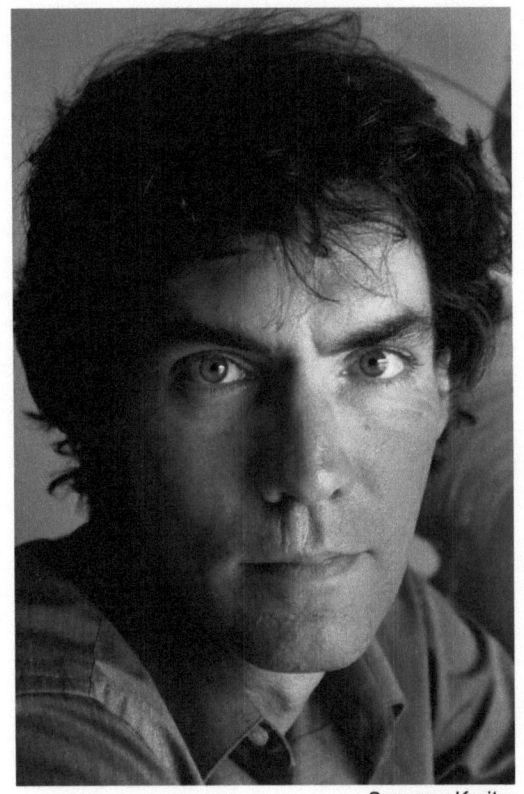

Suzanne Kreiter

Josef Norris is a self-taught painter and mosaic artist. He is the founder and director of Kid Serve Youth Murals. Working with Kid Serve and individually, he has created over 80 outdoor murals in San Francisco and the Bay Area. He lives in San Francisco with his wife and son.

Josef Norris' work can be seen on his website at: www.josefnorris.com
Kid Serve Youth Murals can be reached at: www.kidserve.org